Returning Home

A Collection of Poems from Around the World

“Returning Home, A Collection of Poems from Around the World”

Illustrations: Tracey Bingham of Timaru, Aotearoa
Cover and interior Design: Nuno Moreira, NMDESIGN

Library of Congress Control
Number: 2020916403
ISBN: 978-1-7353818-2-4

Returning Home

A Collection of Poems from Around the World

Ryan J. Kemp

This book is dedicated to my family without whom none of my traveling would've been possible. Thank you for always being there throughout the years in a loving, supportive and accepting way.

We can attempt to remove the variables of our lives and the complications that come with them, but realistically even the difficult parts were perfect as is; because they led us to here, now.

This journey, or this yatra is a journey back to the Heart, back home. Every step we take is leading us back there, whether we know it or not. May we all have a blessed journey home.

R.J.K.

TABLE OF CONTENTS

Note: None of these poems in this book are in chronological order. The time period that these were written within spans from 2013 - 2020.

Chapter 1: Europe

The majority of the poems in this section were written in a transitional time of my life during the fall of 2017. Not that all times aren't transitional when you get used to changing. There are also a few other poems from 2019 which were written on a six week-trip to Italy.

In regards to the earlier poems, such as in Scotland and Germany, I had recently departed Queensland, Australia after separating from my partner of over 3 years.

I was planning on returning to Hawai'i under the premise that I would be drifting my way across Europe and through India and Nepal en route to Myanmar to start working to build solar micro-grids in rural villages there in the hopes that the people could take their power back (literally) from the rapid urbanization that is crippling our planet, deteriorating traditional cultures and languages as people flock to the cities. This planned trip would be enabling the CEO of the renewable energy business I was working for at the time, extra space to raise project finance to launch our endeavors there and put me on salary. The goal was to motorcycle around the country, find sites to set up solar on, work with villagers to assist in micro-grid development for agriculture as well as plant mangrove trees along the Bay of Bengal to combat deforestation with a certain percentage of profits.

Just before leaving to Europe, I had painted my parent's house over the summer when I returned from a trip to Cuba to make a little bit of money. I had driven a Subaru that my cousin gifted me, from Boston to Colorado and once in Colorado, I flew to California & I drove with my good brother from San Francisco on a road trip up through Mount Shasta, Crater Lake and Seattle to Vancouver, BC where I then flew out to Glasgow.

When I left Boston I probably had around three thousand dollars, and that was supposed to make it 4 months across three continents to arrive by the first days of the new year to begin this new work in Myanmar. But, that never came to fruition.

Our realities are in continuous flux yet there is something never changing; the paradox of constancy in change. Planning, to some degree, has always been a futile exercise for me, attempting to extrapolate where I would be at what time and what I would be doing. Living in the moment and following the signs seems to always create an adventure, and our lives are one.

As I re-read these words now, it appears they come from a place of loneliness and desired human connection, finding purpose, potential, surrender and moving on. Enamored with the world, the endlessness of love, and all of the possibilities it can offer.

When I Pass You and You Pass Me

Neukölln, Berlin, Germany

When I pass you and you pass me
Will we ever know what was to be?
Could I see something that you couldn't see?
When I passed you and you passed me

Will we ever know if it was Love at first sight?
Or if the timing just wasn't right?
When we zip by each other like power lines on the train,
Or a quick-shot glance at a homeless man left out in the rain

Maybe we liked the same hot sauce,
Or both liked to camp in rain forests covered in moss.
Maybe we both leave things down to the wire,
Hiding things from each other of what we truly desire

Maybe our grandparents were born in the same town,
Or we both want to plant seeds deep into the ground,
To grow and to fruit like papaya and lime,
I could share with you some moments if you could trade me some time

When I pass you and you pass me,
All these things are left unseen.
But that's how it is in the big, fast world,
Where people barely notice the whirl

Wind blows and leaves fall, did you notice it's cold?
Would I live longer than you if we both were to grow old?
Come along for the ride we can slip and sideways slide,
Let the crow hop alongside and be our Spirit guide

Maybe we can sip coffee down near the Spree,
We can dance around fires naked, wild and free!
Dip into the ocean as the sun slowly sets,
Cut loose all the dolphins from the fishing nets

I thought I saw a twinkle in your eye,
A sparkler, a beam of light that shot through your sky.
But, maybe it was the sun and you have a son,
Maybe it's true, you're not "the one"

When I pass you and you pass me,
My mind falls in this trap so easily.
If it's meant to happen then all shall be still,
If that even's a thing, and not just free will.

The Love That Remains

Drumnadrochit, Scotland

The Love that remains,
Like morning dew;
A memory of the damp night,
That has slipped across the Earth's tilt.
Glistening, the green grass,
Like long lost stars, burnt out millennia ago.

The Love that remains,
Like memories of Grandmother's lap;
Distant yet recalled upon memory's laneways.
Emotive responses to imagery, scents and touch,
Yet no longer here in this place, but still alive in time.

The Love that remains,
Like rings on a tree;
Circling the ages,
But leaving the experiences somewhat hidden.
Who knows what they've seen?
and how they've felt?

The Love that remains,
Like castle ruins on the loch shore;
Relaying feats of triumph and defeat,
Hidden in the stones.
Treaded upon by foreigners to the land and the inherent meaning,
Seeking instantaneous snapshots of understanding.

The Love that remains,
Like wild blackberries dotting the ground;
Not consumed by bird nor man,
But reproductive by Nature of itself.
Continuing its lineage from ground to sky,
Effortlessly, when the time is right.

The Love that remains,
Like faith after failure;
Trust in a higher power and process,
More than ourselves,
Yet one in the same creation.
Witnessing the ripples in the pond,
As the water.

The Key to the Loch

Luss, Scotland

Life's current is that of the flow of the river;
Swiftly moving forward,
Relenting for no one.

Does the river ever look back?
Can even a cold, harsh winter stop the water from running?
Maybe on the surface.
But the underneath continually changes.
Polishing stones,
Quenching the thirst of the beings that sip from it,
The roots that cling to it.

Can you embrace this flow?

Know,
That it is all that is
And that ever was.

Constancy in change,
Form in movement.

Yet,
Truly malleable and formless.
Like Truth,
Many tributaries and brooks,
One ocean.
Connected at the source.

Like a wild horse,
I roam the fields of eternity.
Searching for nothing.

Nothing that is not already inside of me,
Which is everything.

Cocoon

Kreuzberg, Berlin, Germany

When one is born,
They do not choose
Their wings.

Yet,
They have an inner knowing,
Of their ability to fly.

Where will they go?
The sky is so big!
The winds are so strong!
Uncharted territory,
For many.

Upon departure,
The first flight is
Utter freedom.
New sights, smells & colors.
Danger seems to lurk around every corner.

But,
What is life without the risk of death?
What is the meaning of home
If you've never left?

The return to Oneself,
In space or time,
Is but the flap of the soul's wings
In song and rhyme.

The cocoon of home,
Calls out,
In silence.

Eyes on the Street
Prague, Czech Republic

I feel like I'm looking for your eyes on the street
In passer-byes and people that I meet
Comparing how they laugh with how you used to smile
But it is like contrasting documents of a different file

I wonder if your feeling the same thing
Or if you've already forgotten the love we could bring

I showed someone a picture of us the other day
And they said
We looked good together.

If I didn't break the framework
Maybe it could've lasted forever

We could've figured it out like we always did
We could have waited in time to see when we could have a kid
We could've figured it out like it was supposed to happen.

We could've make it work,
I was willing to try
And for a few days when you told me I can't visit I felt like I could die
Because I realized that I'll never have you again like I once had you

I'm lost,
And I don't know where to start
Because for the last few years you've had my Heart
And it felt protected and constant
In these times of change

Now I can't call you when I want to talk
Or mail you thinks I find on the sidewalk
And I want to ,
but it seems you don't want me to do it

And I miss you
Like no one has before

And I miss you
Like the knob misses the door
When they're detached
I feel like I cannot open

Yet hopefully this all shall pass,
Like a ladybug climbing over blades of grass

And I miss you now, more than ever
Sitting on these cobblestones in Prague
Letting rain hit my head trying to wash out the fog
Ran out of grog even though I know it hurts my body
But the pain seems less when I'm in that haze
Absinthe & the green muse veils my eyes from the lonely days
Where I sit alone and sip coffee at two tabled cafés

Although I kind of understand that we can't be together now
And I said that it's fine when you're not around
I can't help but think it is not the right way down

The man in Salem with tarot cards said we were soul mates
And that all is good when we're apart but together it's great
And that at this point he thinks we will be inseparable

But I guess sometimes people need a few years
To remember something lost in all of their fears
Of living in the future or in "what if" land
Letting these beautiful shells slip by in an hourglass of sand

Remembering

Ataturk Airport, Istanbul, Turkey

Our Soul is a treasure, within a chest.
Our chest.
Here there are hidden riches beyond belief.
This treasure has been placed in a desert.
Sandstorms and winds have buried this treasure chest deep.
Deep beneath the sands of time.
The sands of engrained mind-sets,
Sands of judgment.
In this desert, there are wars being ravaged on the sands above the treasure.
Wars of ego,
And wars of expectation.
Wars of the mind that are reflected in the physical reality of our current world.
We,
Who have been so lucky to experience education
And we,
Based on our pathless paths,
Have Remembered that these deserts
Once held a treasure chest with riches beyond belief.
Nevertheless,
To get to this chest,
We must first stop the war.
We must see that the war is a figment of our own imaginations.
Now, with awareness and access to this desert,
We become archeologists of the Soul.
Slowly, gently brushing away sand from on top of this treasure chest.
Slowly, dusting off our potential for internal riches and true universal wealth.
Slowly, stroke by stroke,
We remember this treasure.
This treasure is our Soul,
And we,
Our own archaeologists of it.
We have our own answers if we decide to seek.

Once we see glimpses of this treasure,
It helps us remember who we are,
What we are here to do
& How we are of service.
Holding the welfare of others who have not yet found their treasure,
or don't know where to look.
Progenitors.
Archaeologists of the soul vision,
Excavators of the universal mind,
Uncovering and remembering why.
Why we are who we are,
Why we look the way we look,
Our skills,
Our mistakes,
And steps we have taken to arrive
Here,
Now.
Dusting off the treasure,
That is buried deep within all of us.
Remembering.

Unraveling

Maremma, Tuscany, Italy

Some people have told me they don't feel inspired to travel.
Well, do you like eating plain chicken and white rice your whole life?
And by traveling I don't mean touring.
I mean unraveling.
Traveling is for the mind and spirit as spices and different cuisine are for the palette; completely taking over your senses and sense of self,
helping you to morph and shift into the depths of your own humanity
and the diversity that represents it.
Histories envelop you,
myths you never knew existed can resonate and shift your understanding,
symbols you've never seen can become impressed on your mind
all because of the power they empower within you.
You can recognize complete strangers,
these strangers can become your family,
and this family can become your community.
You can see and hear birds you never knew existed,
smell flowers you've never smelled
& glimpse divine beauty that inspires artists like Michelangelo, Rafael and Da Vinci.
You Can run in the rain to a brewery on a hill
looking over ancient Etruscan grounds,
fertile with legend and life.
To not discover is depriving your genes their conditioned expression.
Only as of recent in human evolution have we stopped moving and constantly learning about our home.
In times of change learners inherit the earth;
while the learned find themselves beautifully equipped
to deal with a world that no longer exists.
In other words, you could be in Cotonou under the full moon learning voodoo,
or you could be in your office eating a cup full of noodles & a YooHoo.
Who chooses?
Material fades faster than experience.
Experience fades faster than integration.

Integration fades faster than wisdom.
Wisdom doesn't fade.
The world will survive even if humanity decides to lose its race.
What are we running towards in the first place?
Who are we competing against?
The clock stops no matter what.
Time slows when you're off of it,
in the primordial dot of exploration of your own self through the external world.
Be. Hold.

No Justice, No Peace
Milan, Italy

No justice, no peace
No farms, no feed
We're pathless, no feets
Adjust to defeat
Walk in what you seek
Many ways to the peak
Get a peep of the creek
It meanders and leaks
Sprouting leeks, feeding beaks
Like a snake without sneak
We inherit the meek
Instead of milling the teak
Protect the ceiling, jah keep
And Jah guide crownless sheiks
Undiscovered mystiques
It takes weeks to get weak
This bless-ed physique
Quilted soul like batik
Map u to Mozambique
This aint no newspeak
You can find in Newsweek
The technique is unique
Here's a kiss from my cheek

Chapter 2: United States of America

From San Diego to Cahokia, New Hampshire to Idaho, I have roamed a large expanse of the United States of America, which is such a vast country of beautiful, sacred land and interesting dynamics of human beings.

The time and the place of all of these poems is extremely varied. It is hard to summarize in an introduction of where these poems have come from. Ultimately, I feel that the place often designates the information that comes out of me. Like an antenna picking up a specific frequency of the location, certain poems just come out. In addition, many of these poems were inspired by images I may have seen written on the sidewalk, or the name of the lake that I was near, or a flower on the side of the road that stood out from the other flowers.

For example, the poem entitled 'Temptation' was inspired when my friend Brian and I were walking in Chicago near Montrose Beach close to Lake Michigan and we went walking through an underpass tunnel. In the tunnel there was a bright red apple that as just sitting there, and it felt surreal. The poem flowed out soon thereafter.

Some sort of nuance in the environment almost always enabled these poems to flow out in that regard as they exposed nuances in my experience. This is one of the reasons I feel that traveling is so profound. As we are all energetic beings living on the energetic being of the Earth. When we are in certain places, the energy of the place (which has been documented in ley lines for example) comes through, plays around with our beings and we change. Sometimes, various information is exchanged and is manifest in so many different ways depending on our own diversity.

Celebrated
Carlsbad, California

Go where you are celebrated
For your colors and uniqueness
Not merely tolerated for being a flower

We are all soil dwelling
And oxygen breathing
Moving towards the light

Our wild winds wafting with one another
Connecting our plumes into one piece of mastery
Like the Aurora Borealis

A layer of protection
Healing us from the disconnection
Sealing us from the harshest realities of space

Right above our ceiling
And dealing us the most magic hand
That the Magi have ever seen

To be alive in this lucid dream
Of perfect rainbow steam
Off the river's water gleam

The sun beams
From the raven's eye
Guiding and gliding amongst the skies
Guarding us and perceiving without a question why

We are all
Just a twinkle
A wrinkle
In cosmic rhyme

So celebrate!
For you are a unique you
And deserve your own ceremony
To be celebrated

Fuck your Phone!

NYC, New York

Fuck your phone
Keep your head up!
People walking into each other
Speaking to ghosts
The world is here,
It's that one you're stepping on.
Not that blue-light-lit veil of comparison
And illusion.
You may like being
Your own psychological magician,
But I'll stick to the slight of Heart,
Wherever our feet meet
On the New York city streets.

Temptation
Chicago, Illinois

Temptation comes in many forms
Luscious and red
Like lipstick polluted sky
And the freshly painted nails of a temptresses' eye

Nature's seductions
Our mind's echo chamber pulsates with Heart's percussion
We can enjoy our own prisons
When they are filled with comfort
Halls of mirrors with chandeliers and chartreuse paisley wallpaper
Corpses dressed in costumes walking to the banquet hall
Having a ball

The serpent lives inside our tall grasses
Slithering silently amidst the swamps
And mangroves

If the apple doesn't fall far from the tree
How did I become me?
From whom are these seeds?

The soil is sometimes too acidic for
The soul's alkalinity
The vanity
Like a manatee
Causing internal calamity

Humility
Could be as simple as validating
Another's humanity

Lilith saw
Adam's jaw
And dropped out like a paw paw

Letting dawn turn to early Eve
And dusk into Spirit sieve

The colors bleed like ink on papyrus
So does the virus
But without the temptation we cannot see the Truth
Juxtaposed staring at each other in telephone booths
Calling in one calls in the other
Can there be a father without a mother?
It's fine to flaunt with the temptress
But don't let her smother

Storm

Great Sands Dunes, Colorado

You'll never do anything if you depend on the weather
Storms come and go
Like birds of a feather
Flock whenever
We're wheeled in this forever.

Until we see the clouds and the rain as blessing
Not even in disguise
We become divert of the lies
Like streams with big rocks
Time with no clocks
Wealth with no stocks
Feet with no socks

Up the sand dunes during the lightning
It weeds out the prunes
Wrinkled up from Looney Tunes they absorb
Through the tube like food
We all consume
But are we aware of our consumption?
That soap
That friend
That whatever sum'n sum'n

In that storm, keep walking
When the message ain't received, keep chalking
Not everyone's ready for the things that we're talking

Sun's out
Thunder's gone
Only a few standing strong
The rest are holed up in their cars singing songs
About their wishes that they had stood out in the drizzle
Just lasted a bit longer than the collective sheep whistle

So they could've witnessed the storm sweep in on the peaks
If you are what you walk, then you are what you seek

A Message from the Driftwood

Gustavus, Alaska

If the driftwood tree says, "Hello"
Sitting on the beach
Are you ready
To hear what it shall teach?

Jellyfish seaweed in the nook
Stillness by the water
Glacial stone in my palm
Do no harm
Stand strong
We're the mountain's sons and daughters

The water is calling
The name 'Heen' it knows
Traveling through time
The cosmos and the snows
Living, breathing Earthen
The elves they need to serve and
The wisdom's impacts steep
Rooted in the deep

The waves communicating
Love to the shore it's making
Not the same love you gotta
Throw into the oven and bake-in
Like bacon

The pig is loving you
Do you give it back the Love
It deserves to have too?
Baloo
The bare necessities are what we leave in order
Support her
The bear calls out to

Protect the world
And turn her

Around in your mind
Make us all press rewind
Remembering all the times
When we let time unwind
Now blind
Some are of those that walk this precious planet –

We ran it
We walked it
We moved it
We talked it
Unlocked it
The locket
A sprocket of patience
Of over-standing way beyond
Each and all our measures

The pleasure of living
Lies in the strawberries
We rolling out now
Thinking light, becoming heavy

Alignment

Auke Bay, Alaska

Alignment
All in perfect timing
The stripes swiped with lies
And
His story just rhymes
With the victors reclining
On the backs of other's decline
More and more the light shines
As we're constantly reminded
By the bystanders miming
Lining all up in line
To lie down like swine
Slaughtered and sipped with the wine
Apple in mouth
Backs facing behind
This Faceless paradigm
It's time to end this crime
Sweep up the grime
Like Summer Sander's slime
And repair the Hearts and minds
Through collaborative design
Healing intertwined
Like DNA twine
Banyan tree vines rooted in sunshine
Divine lunchtime
Every time
Any time
We climb summits sublime
Even and prime
Einstein
The singing bowl chimes
Walking us into the Dreamtime
That we can walk with shining defiance
And define our own shrine

Water and Rocks

Pacific Grove, California

Emotion is normal
Like water flowing in to the rocks
We are channels
Vessels
It laps up against their sides
Spraying mist
Seagulls caw
And dodge and dive in mid-air
Mussels grow on the rock faces
And the water flows out

Do the rocks cling to the water's flow?
No
They stoically sit
In their rock-ness
Gazes locked
Frozen in time like the Loch Ness
Seaweed buckling and popping
Rising and falling
Like breath

Life
Death
Without clinging
It can be so easy.
When the breeze
Brings the salt back in,
There it is again

Co-create > Co-destroy

Big Sur, California

Co-create rather than co-destroy
The intention is the joy
You trying to prove your own point?
Or help the other grow?

Forests burn
With the understanding of destruction to heal.
But the deal
Is creation
Transformation takes patience
And as all us awakening patients
Slowly go ape-shit
We all start to face it
Defacing conditions that used to speak
Where our face is
Responsibility for our Home
And the sentiments of all sentients alone
But never gone
Where we gon' run to?

I see one path that's True
And it's back to me through You
We toe the middle way through

Wondering About Wonder

Skagway, Alaska

I wonder what wonder costs?
What is really lost during loss?
You gain the world but lose your socks
Barefoot we gon-go
Who you gon' run to
When the Earth can't take it no more?

Get Rich or Try Sharing

Chicago, Illinois

Get rich or try sharing
It's daring
To be different

To be you
In a world that's confused
Babylon strung along halls
Of walls and flashing lights
And mirrors
Making the divine reflection feel dimmer
The more it shimmers
The more normalcy is honored
By these monoculture farmers
Continuing to plant
Ecocidal trauma

Where's the lama?
They twist the Bible and the words of a Prophet
For profit
Make you crave her hips and lips
Until you're sexually repressed
Embarrassed to get undressed
When you finally find the one who passed Jah test
I peacefully protest
This lack of unrest!

With these words I drool
Spinning language spools
Go to the village, fool
See who's really got the tools
If sea level rises
And you're so surprised
Because you didn't prepare
And consumed all the lies

Who in their right mind
Gon' take you in
If your value ain't shit
Without a keyboard and a politicized grin?

The Now is in
Eating cows is a sin
But we can keep going
Samsara is all knowing
Like Santa Claus ho-ho'ing
Can't escape without glowing
From the inside we're growing
Like flower petals flowing
On the Ganga

Light your own lamp
Nurture it with a sangha
Integrate
Figure eight
Pound Malanga
Susquehanna Arcana
Grandma got the grammar
No sickle, no hammer
Just forty-two gammas
And some trees like bananas

Foliage

Mount Willard, New Hampshire

To be done trying
It is a beautiful dying
The compost of your own soul

Transitionary
The in-between season states
Knowing no-thingness

Nothing more to prove
Could hang 'em up
Or root 'em down

A merry-go-round
When the leaves come down
Will you be near or around

To walk on the ground?
Sacrifice one things
And another thing will die
Will it be reborn?

Does the river flow
With the intention to quench
The thirst of the land?

Or it meanders
In the gravity and way
That it merely does?

Does purpose evolve?
Or is it a constructed
Figment of ego?

We crave to be seen

To be heard and to share things
From what depths they rise?

Inward we will turn
To see things we don't want to
Outward we then go

Only time will tell
What direction the wind sweeps in
Across the chasm

Pa(rentals)
La Jolla, California

Miracles Born of a thought initially instinctual
An ocean of fertility, navigated by divine paddles
Harmonious union of beings in hue-man form
Love sparkles warm light through the storm
We're born into this water world
Blank canvas, bright eyes, unknown smiles
Nurtured by nature and clinging to love
Without knowing what it is

Energy fields floating around,
Warm affections shown, twenty-four-hour-grown and unconditional emotion

Complete attention diverted from the external to us
Living only because they planted us in their desire for blossoming life

Time passes,
Cerebral classes mold ideas and dreams into ours'
Sands trickle, forming hills of thought without a notion of what to think
Formed before we know we are formless

Tick tock, money spent, adventures shared
Sometimes taking for granted all those who care
Not realizing we are them, mini-stitches in a wider hem
Landed in this world from other realms, purposely placed here, now.

Explorations of the mind lead to weakened holds of certain ideas
Glimpsing their eyes and seeing our selves
Having survived on their wealth and building our own
Starting from ground trying to get back home

The realization of the value of the priceless
Infinite love given, where has the time went?
Pre-pubescent identity theft recovered at the peak

Of sun drenched mountains, ocean view, voiceless speak

I love you so much I can't even describe
Although I don't say it all the time
I'm learning to see from this new set of eyes
How many feathers you put into these wings meant to fly

Your blessings infinitely looping through me
As I breath, as I blink, as I think, as I be
Contently content in your lap I lay my head
Thoughts free float till my soul awakens from this bodily bed

Until my last breath this adventure is ours together
The impacts we make, interconnected forever
I myself am you, and you yourself are me
It takes all of our love to set all of us free
Thank you

Earth Day

San Francisco, California

Mother Earth bears the fruit for all of us to share,
Miracles of all colors and shapes she does bear.
She gives them away freely, yet she's still well aware,
Of the changing of the times, the sound floats in the air.

Some things they are changing, perhaps for the worse.
How much more can she give unless the trends are reversed?
It's way past due-time to put Mother Earth first,
To clean up the water before we all desperately thirst.

To clean up the air before our alveoli clog.
To turn transport green, or cough and choke in the smog.
To stop numbing and dumbing our spirits with grog.
To allow the phoenix of Spirit to rise in Love from the bog.

Do we wade in the fields that are rolling in green?
Or do we sit on the pavement made with black oil's sheen?
Do we go to the farm and learn to plant the green bean?
Or do we keep methane pumping with carcass cuisine?

How long do we have until the point of no return?
How much longer will it take until we all finally learn?
That to this task we as One Heart all must rise.
And stop abusing Mother Earth, that is, before she dies

Guest

La Promenade Café, Outer Richmond, San Francisco, CA

I thoroughly enjoy being a guest in every place that I go to.
An anonymous face,
Simply passing through;
Knowing a few people,
Or connecting with new ones,
Joining them on local activities and small gatherings,
And then I'm gone.

Ethereal footprints,
Walking the desolate streets of Balboa
On crisp Monday mornings.
The park in view off towards the right,
Only a few hooded faces on the sidewalk bearing the breeze,
And two cats peering out of the window at me.

A bank security member,
Smiles gleefully as we simultaneously say "Good Morning" to one another,
Validating our shared existences on this plane,
As I continue to the La Promenade Café
To acquire some warmth mixed with caffeine.

It's a viewpoint, a perspective,
To always be a guest,
And always be a host.
In the shapes of the ever changing street-scapes,
Restaurants, coffee houses,
Trees in bloom or in decline,
Time weaves divine.

Everything is new,
And that's how I like it;
Wonder full,
Connected,
And alone.

The sun & I,
Shining together.

We Must Give to Receive (in Memory of Nora the Chicken)
San Antonio, Texas

It takes life to give life
In all things we do
The efforts we present
The waters that we knew

A living being's breath we take
To nourish ourselves
Is pure breath in itself
Our cells inward it delves

The plants grow up to the sky
As the worms go down
Symbiotic relations
The whole world round

But it seems when we take life
There's no recognition of such
No respect given, no honor
No gratitude, or at least, not much

For the gifts of this life
At the top of the food chain, so we think
Believing this tenderloin strip
Just came from the factory sink

To take a breath away yourself
Leaves you skipped Heart, lack of air
Gasping in recognition
Of the life that was just, once there

This blood is our blood
We flow together as one
This flesh given to us
Not caloric intake for fun

Every action we take
Utilizing the life of another
Is a reflection back in the eyes
Of ourselves and the mother

Take away one organism on Earth
A chain reaction occurs
Take away human presence
You may even hear the birds

The forests will echo
Speaking back their Love songs
And the animals will flourish
Just as they belonged

Not exploiting and taking
Feeling profitable as key
The duality half left open
Wide gaping eyes that can't see

The Ouroboros hiss
The Toroid enveloping
The sacred geometry of life
For our interplanetary developing

As I look into the sun
Eyes burning with glee
With our powerful life-force
Looking straight back at me

What do you give back?
What do you intend to receive?
Why are you living the way you are?
Is there a seed in the leaves?

Of your rustling soul
Floating free in the wind?

Every smile we flash
A potential new friend

Or an old reconnection
From past-life contracts signed
Thousands of pebbles rippling the pond
Combining in time's sublime rhyme

Speaking Love to the plants
That you grow in the yard
Sending Love to your family
Whether near, whether far

The strings behind the scene
Unseen by the mean
Unless you take a close look
Sense your frequencies gleam

We must give to receive
Equilibrium's plot
Giving without expectation
Judgement free of the knots

We must learn to be
And be to learn
The contradictory art
Of past learning wheel turns

The giver in me
Is the receiver in you
But the Love in us all
Is what's infinite and True

Heart > Head

San Francisco, California

When head gives way
To Heart
All shall be revealed

As layers drop off
To be refocused,
Like an onion peel.

Balal,
The Aramaic root of the word 'Babylon'
Means to confuse

The Heart
Brings clarity
Beyond the ruse

Synchronicity

Sedona, Arizona

Synchronicity
Drapes over me
Like a willow tree
Looking at the sea

Serendipity
Drips from the skies
Like a sweeping rain
From the hurricane's eye

Love and light
Come shining down
Basking us
In her golden brown

Faith and truth
Will come to me
Come one, come all
Let's all be free!

We Are

Aptos, California

We are a drop of water in an endless rainstorm
Quenching the earth, the plants, the animals and sea
We form the life blood of the planet like a river
Flowing to the vastness of universal dreams

We are the feathers of wings of brother eagle
Flying high above the ground we see how small we are
But we are strong and infinite and humble in our journeys
And we can rise above it all and merge with father sky

We are the constellations spinning high above us
Swirling, twirling, shining- for everyone to see
We thrive in constancy but are forever changing
Playing with the galaxies who shine like stars to be

We are the silken petals of the meadow flower
beautiful and bountiful, lounging in the sun
Colors , shapes and sizes created for survival
Everyone is different yet everyone's the same

We are the glowing embers of the burning fire
Glistening in darkness, smoldering in light
We burn forever if we find our true Loves
Simple elemental manifestations of the One

Blue Jay

Andover, Massachusetts

Blue Jay bouncing outside the window
Telling me to be confident in what I know,
and who I think am.

Revel in the presence that we bring.
The excitement that comes about when it's time to sing
That song from the Heart.
The embracing of life, all its vibrancy and clarity.

To have faith that we are rising in energy.
To use power wisely and don't let others misuse theirs'.
To be conscious and loving
And prepared.

Divine Circus

Gray Whale Cove State Beach, Montara, California

Sitting on the rocks,
The edge of a continental land mass.
Zoom out,
Where am I?
What edge am I sitting on now?
Is it in my power to push these boundaries in a safe manner?

An infinite being
Yet a small witness.
A cell in the planetary organism,
Who can sometimes trap themselves
In a mental cell.

What would happen if a termite
Was infused with the intelligent neural capacity of a human?
It would short circuit.
What would happen if a human
Was infused with the intelligent neural capacity
Of the all pervading creative source?
Would we short circuit?
Would we recognize Jesus if he was walking around today?

These self made boundaries,
Rocky coasts on our journey's continental shelf,
Caused by rapid tectonic plate shifts of consciousness;
Shifts of vibration,
Shifts of resonance,
Are self imposed through our partial free will.

We're participating in the hack,
But are we the hacker?
We can choose to honor spirit, nature and the processes that inherently we are connected with,
Or we can honor mind, distraction and the processes that may lead to dis-

connection from the prior.

Perhaps this is our choice,
Perhaps not.

Zoom back in,
As I sit,
Pensive on the rocks,
Mist kissing my face,
Watching some homies surf,
Assimilating Dopey's gift,
One of the seven dwarfs,
Forest kin.

Winning or losing,
We are always choosing,
If we slip and fall,
We can wipe the slate clean,
And redeem.

Each moment is anew,
And if we only knew
The power we carry within us,
Perhaps we would be open to more activities and wisdom that is constantly warming up our electrical channels and circuits,
For the divine circus.

Snow

Amtrak to Portland, Maine from Haverhill, MA

Snow perforates my vision
As it slowly falls downward.
Kisses from the sky,
A twinkle in her eye.

Trees lightly dusted,
Like history manifest.
Each molecule unique
On the spines of ringed storytellers.

Branches crumble under the weight
Of transmuted life.
Bringing light through death,
& birth through carnage

The weightlessness of the fall,
Within thermals we rise.
It would all be so flight full,
If we were comfortable on the ground below.

The crisp spirit spirals,
Through my inhalation gates.
Reminding me of life
In this miracle of awakening.

& as the snow hits my skin,
It cools the fire within.
Everything in due stride,
No hands on the time.

Clouds don't wait,
For decisions to be made.
They release their tears of joy
On barren lifeless ground.

You can try to bury us
Without realizing we are time capsules.
When the ground is fertile,
We grow how we see.

Guardian Angel

Andover, Massachusetts

Guardian angel
Can you speak to me?
Point out my blind spots that I can't see?
Will you always be here even if I fuck up?
Trip, fall and smash my face on the ground?
What if I don't always acknowledge all the signs you provide?
Or if I hop into a car hitchin' with a drunk ride?
Can I confide in you?
Are you hiding in me?
May we seek each other?

Guardian angel,
I'm praying to you for guidance,
All of these co-incidences
Leading me in circles forward,
Like the ellipses of the Milky Way
Spiraling through the universe
Reverberating plasma through my planetary presence.
I present to you my deepest flaws,
And fears,
Switching gears in chapters of the story,
I hope you're a constant reader who is still engaged as I am engaged in the thought of you.

Guardian angel,
Do you exist in the ether?
Are you teleporting through portals invisible to mortals in combat with themselves?
Sometimes I can sense your eyes on me
And the ears you have in all space
Despite my geographical place
I call on you for protection and grace.

The crash of the ocean, I taste your potion.

The blow of the wind, I feel you within.
The ray of the sun, I hope you're the one.

Leading us back to thee,
Enriching our soils with blood and bone tea,
Soul free.

Guardian angel,
Thank you for all you do,
I know I'm not the easiest to help along through,
But I'm keen and my eyes are open for your calling cards and guide posts,
Man boasts but time claims no such,
But rivers and canyons and rust,
Dust and rolling stone lust,

& Trust.

Lost Dream

Turners Falls, Massachusetts

It feels like a lost dream
That my grip has slipped from as I awaken
Vaseline fingers.

Birds are chirping, the sun is slowly peeking through your window
And the plants are doing their morning stretch on the sill.
But you're not there and your pillow isn't under my arm.

I attempt to remember what the dream was about,
The vivid images and senses that I had just experienced in that other world.
The words and how they tasted moving from my lips to yours and back again.
But it's like rain from a puddle seeping into the Earth.

My mind morphs into a new temporary state of viewing,
As this dream world splinters into the abyss.
I am disoriented with the shift back to this realm;
A lamp flickers, a cat curls next to my foot, purring her love through my film.
There's a half man half tiger painted on the toilet seat near the cat claw tub with the rusty pipes
And an orb changes colors from blue to pink in the hallway.

I miss the dream, I long for the warmth.
I remember it was beautiful and unique and fun and loving.
So why is it so far away?
Where did it go?

Mind's open doors soon swing closed
Nudging me out into a hallway of knobs and keyholes,
As I look into my pockets for the right key
To click in and reconnect me back into my memory.

I remember you by the waves of the endless horizon and sunset.

I remember you on the couch in California near the railroad tracks when I glimpsed your soul.
I remember our walks to the train in the morning as the crows cawed down at us from the Jacaranda trees
But your face is blurred and hard to focus on
My retroactive vision isn't 20:20.

Your smell was so natural,
Your smile so pure,
Your skin so smooth
Your heart I adored.
It was Effortless being together
In our dream.

But now it's hard to remember the feel of your hair,
And the way your eyes lit up a room.
Deep blues and greens with a dark coral reef ring around the iris;
A supernova of beauty exploding in my pupils.

I want to remember,
But maybe you want to forget.
Maybe you're a dream-slate wiper,
Clearing the dream as I awaken;
Like a teacher with an eraser on the chalkboard,
Swiftly preparing for a new lesson by clearing off the old chicken scratch.

It feels strange
In this new world,
Because I know there was an amazing story written on these blank pages once,
In invisible ink
Hidden in the bookshelf with no title on the spine.

I don't want to write over it just yet,
I want to skip to a new ending
Out on page 383.

A page where all is gentle sun rays on Sundays
And turquoise blue waters kiss our skin.
Maybe I'll try to go back to sleep and reclaim this dream within.
Until we meet again.

Leaves in the Sun

Greenfield, Massachusetts

We leaves in the sun,
Blown by the infinite breeze,
Of our Souls searching
& swaying.

Look no further
Than the strong rooted tree
From which you wave.

We emerge and crumble,
Change color and shape,
As the seasons roll past.
All in their own reason
Without treason to the whole.

We think we can muster by trying,
But it is futile to remain still
Against the howling winds.

Release!

The primordial dot,
In the moment that is it,
Without thought,
Opens us and prepares us
For ourselves to begin
Again

Organization

Los Angeles, California

What would every organization look like if people weren't harmed?
If they functioned as healed
Instead of attempting to drain each other's energy to place them on top?
They fueled by connecting their flames
For a larger light
Instead of a forest fire enferno.

Enfermo breeds enfermo
From Los Angeles to Palermo
You know these signs are just posts to guide us to the most of what we are

Enlightened Buddha stars
From Mars and Andromeda
From the hood with the Robins
Breasts and chests
Seeking for treasure
No rest
But the gold ain't physical
It's spiritual
Locked in the Heart
With the key waiting to be seen
Like a gleam of light through the mossy trees
Splaying verdant servants for our own observance

Turn it
Flip the round around
Like a circle's carousel's ground
Never lost, never found
Come back here with me to the Now

Respiration

Santa Cruz, California

Language pulls you from the source
Because it draws you away from the essence of the being or action.
A thought pops in
And assigns the infinite expanse a meaning
Something to derive an understanding though
Rather than the wonder and awe.

When language is transmuted
From a prison
To a prism
We are released from its netted holds
Of conceptuality
Into immortality
Ultimate reality

The moment goes
Beyond stop and go
To and fro
Ebb and flow
Two sides of the same Joe
I suppose

My toes led
Me to the walls
Of Santa Cruz
Christ on the cross
Delivering channeled source
Using this voice

No divisions
Less superstitions
The spirits are here
When we go clear
Not Scientology fear

The conditions are real
And as we pull back the peel
Insides the fruit.
The more you eat the more you scoot
Directionally, conventionally
Con cave and convectionally
Just depends on the food you consuming
Like oodles of Noodling
From my medulla drools

The waves are talking
Birds are walking
And we're trying to record it all
Chalking
Despite the impermanence of the clocking.

Leave it in time
Before it rewinds
Backwards and forward in lime-light supernova
Cosmic shaken bottle soda
One iota in continua
I'ma continue-tah
Open up as a channel for me and
You
Both bruh
And sister

That my mission to the vision
We trapped in this together
Do you see what I'm sipping?
Let's share it
And connect to cheers to the rest
Of these breaths

Alōha
Presence and space sharing
No quota

In love
Dove flies above the doors to my eyes
Deer stand beside
Dolphin pods come
Seals coax me to swum
Pelican leaves the skin
From within
To remind me of grin
Cosmic shin, shine like
Rhyme and thyme
Sprinkled Mime

Attract whom
Your Moon
Unit revolves to
That Love can't be bought
No matter how many rises or falls we were taught

And so it all is as it blooms
Gaia and Luna
Dancing in tune
To the vacuum

Full circle
Circulation
Respiration

Ponies in the Mist

Greenfield, Massachusetts

Two ponies in the mist
Don't get it twisted
We all decay
But we never fade away

We come back to the same spot
To se if we take the same direction
The pathways ever changing
The routes we trot, re-arranging

Two horses in the fog
Never forget
That the forgetting is remembering
That the acceptance is dismembering

The traumas that have folded
To be unfolded
And lain bare like fern canopy

To sprout afresh
Untrammeled
Anew

River
Moab, Utah

The river is a memory
The river holds memory
The river is our brother
The river is our sister
It weaves us through time
It weaves us through space

The raven flies by
The moon hangs high
The rocks dusty red burning glow
Tears come like Melting snow
The fire of the valley warms my heart
Helps me remember where to start

The rapid's sides on which I've ambled
The bushes green and thicket brambles
The rocks look out with faces proud
Of lineages of power all around

The wind it kisses me cold on the cheek
Of parts once lost, for which we weep
Of parts pushed down by pressures strong
We can never give up to get along
If you listen close you can hear the song
Sing along, sing along

Vulnerability

Crater Lake NP, Oregon

The craters in our heart
Only harm the ones we love
Because we haven't fully loved ourselves

This lake never can be filled until we do
It's depths, the deepest of the deep
The clearest of the clear

When we freeze the flow of water into it
Our shells implode, like Mt. Mazama
Leaving a gaping hole

And the crater remains empty, lonely
Looking for others to fill us up
We give and we give

As we only crave our own love
The crater is waiting for us!

Perhaps if we can accept this
we would stop trying to defend ourselves
And let our guard down

Echo

Echo Lake, California

You can come along
We can all sing the same songs
Just like an echo

You can stay alone
The trees and the birds are there
Just like an echo

We call to ourselves
Through the rocks, cliffs and the lakes
We are an echo

Time reverberates
It collapses and expands
In the do'ers hands

I am here today
And insofar, gone 'morrow
In the whispering

We are happening
Like the wind, sky and the clouds
Just like an echo

Zoom In

Nantucket, Massachusetts

I've stopped chasing the present
And as I've stopped running
The present becomes what it is
No need to seek
No need to stress
Like a rocking chair it gives us something to do
But gets us nowhere

Where I am going is not something I can see
It is not somewhere I can go
It is when all of that comes to a natural cessation
And there is nothing more to do

The times of stillness are the spaces of growth
The times of inflection are the spaces of reflection
Every moment out of alignment is in the process of alignment
Zoom out on the vantage point
And then zoom back in.

Hollow Eyes

San Francisco, California

It's been buried in their Hearts for a long time
You can see it in their hollow eyes,
Longing for connection.

Now, even their mouths are covered
So you can't hear their silent screams.

We reach out for connection
Only to be snuffed by the dense concrete

People are ungrounded in the cities,
For there is no ground.

A mind-vacuum
A soul in a flickering streetlight
A pandemic of seriousness
That tips the scales of desperation.

The coffee is stronger
The air is thicker
The streets are hotter, with a passion
That longs to burn for something that matters.

The longing is for themselves!
This schism between mind and Heart
Leaves a vacuous chasm that cannot be blocked by any levy,
Lower 9th style.

Mosquitoes and stock piles
Peppermint and old tiles
Sharp eyes and cutting smiles

Angel, relax a while
Don't you know you're divine?

We've been doing this all since the beginning of time
Let that take some pressure off
It's always been cyclically rhymed
Kick back and just sit awhile
Get back to the lemons and limes
You'll be fine
You'll be fine.

The Predator

Greenfield, Massachusetts

We are dropped into this jungle of life
& immediately told to run.
Run for your life! Don't look back!
Have you ever looked around and thought,
Why is everybody running?

Everyone is jumping through low-hanging vines,
Dodging roots,
Leaping over quicksand pits,
Judo-chopping Anacondas.

Where is everyone running?
Maybe there are a few who are jogging,
Or even some who are walking,
Crinkling the leaves up in their hands,
And smelling the sweet aromas that are released.
Outliers; the few and far between.

Who told us all to run?
What's waiting for me at the end of the race?
What am I going to do when I get there?
Am I enjoying the run itself?
Should I slow down? Speed up?
Some people got a head start - that's not fair!
What am I leaving behind?

We try to angle the run,
Picking up coins like Mario,
Saving them for some energy boost,
Or to dish some to Luigi to buy a new whip and pick up Peach for their date at the Rainbow rollercoaster.

Caffeine- zoom!
Alcohol - relax!

Cocaine - sprint!
Ganja - don't worry, be happy!

Running is tough on the body,
But more so, grueling on the mind.
Rushing through the jungle, barely realizing what we're doing.
Did you see that Flying Squirrel?
Did you smell that Jasmine flower?
Did you taste that ripe fig that was gifted from the canopy to the jungle floor?

We're on such high alert all the time,
It's like we are escaping from a predator.
Running from our own death,
Towards our own death,
All at the same time.
Why do you think time goes so fast?

Could it be possible,
That "questioning" itself, in why we're running in the first place,
Is the predator we are trying to escape?
What if we find we have no good answers to the important questions we raise?

Most thought schools prize answers over questions,
Answers are believed to provide ways to solve problems,
Move ahead, give guidance, improve life.
Knowing the right questions is hard to ask,
So we rely on others expertise.

Off the shelf self help,
Some curated life style yelp.
One size doesn't fit all,
Questioning can make you feel small,
Humility doesn't mean you can't stand tall.

Perhaps life is a procession,

A ceremony,
An ecstatic dance,
A morning swim,
A blink of an eye,
One breath in the the divine lungs,
Of time.

The Experiential Mirror

Greenfield, Massachusetts

One can only comprehend things truly
That they have experienced directly.
How to contemplate jealousy
If you've never been overtaken with envy?
What does that feel like?

Can I contemplate hunger,
If I've always had adequate food,
Or at least the means to buy some if I got too starving?

Is it possible to know ecstasy,
Without losing yourself in a moments' embrace?

How to be compassionate if you've never felt overflowing empathy in action?
Can we be respectful if we've never been shown respect?
Are the depths of another's sadness accessible by someone who has never been in their exact position at the exact same time?

The mirroring affect calls us into the center of experience;
Where outer and inner worlds connect.
The origination point of infinite kinetics,
A mind without phonetics.

Mirrors are so personal!
Almost vain, depending on how you use them.
Often we don't value whom or what helps us to expose
The stained and rusted areas of our own mirrors.
They make us feel things we haven't felt before,
Dissonant and cringe-worthy at our last actions,
Because perhaps we were the inflictors of such feelings to another.

Easier to do it than having it done to you.
These people, peep-hole our hypocrisy,
Help to humble us and help us recognize our laxity of compassion.

We must be effortful and skillful in our pursuit of recognition of all others within us!
The alacrity to hop on one another in this dog-eat-dog mentality only widens the Illusory cavity of separation between all living family.

A Dock to Nowhere
Harpswell, Maine

A dock to nowhere
We are all trying to sail
But we are the boat

Docked in our own minds
Waiting for the wind to blow
And show us the way

Star navigation
Led by the constellations
Of our Heart and Soul

Then the wind picks up
Are we equipped to go sail?
When is the next gust?

Bob like the buoy
Fluorescent in the Grey clouds
Floating is easy

Inlets are rocky
Steering is more fun this way
Maybe we could crash

Leafless trees still live
Waiting for their leaves to come
When the time is right

We don't need to try
The light does all of the work
Orange turns to green

We are here right now
To be guided by the breeze

Taught by the waters

Undo the slip knot
A dock to infinity
Just loosen the reigns

Some People
Nantucket, Massachusetts

Some people calculate minutes of the day
Some people plan their life away
Instead of going with the flow
They dam it, block it, frame it so

Some people driving fancy cars
Dressed to the 9s in fancy bars
They pin their worth where maggots dwell
And separate their soul, afar

Some people know so many things
About rocks and stocks and shiny rings
They stack the facts like library shelves
And confuse the concept with the king

Some people watch the hours' tick
I'm seeing life-times out 8 clicks
Just trying to find the link to time
Forgetting to remember wakes me quite quick

Some people are really shouting out
Forgetting silence has the loudest mouth
So forced the voice directing choice
Away from those who scream and shout

Some people cruise the Tesla quick
They floss like dentists, span and spick
But float adrift the sheep'll sprint
And corral themselves, no flint to flick

Some people seem to be quite lost
Like new moon night amidst the frost
Yearning deeply for the heat to come
Yet tomorrow looms and moments, toss

Some people help me see myself
The judgments that we cast, a-stealth
We navigate our own minds through
To depths like Marianas shelf

We dive and dive and slowly see
The shore where we have always been
That stood underfoot the entire time
As waves pull back from sand to sea

Aren't We All?

Nantucket, Massachusetts

Aren't we all music?
Aren't we all souls?
Aren't we all captured
In our beautiful fish bowls?

And aren't we all just frequency?
Aren't we all just love?
Aren't we all the wars combined
And aren't we all the doves?

Aren't we all pure pleasure
And aren't we all pure pain?
Do not we love the sunset?
Do we not love the rain?

And aren't we all just spirit?
Don't we all just breathe?
Aren't we all seeking purpose?
Having our wants and our needs?

Aren't we all just human?
Don't we all just bleed?
We all are eating transmuted light
We all want to do and to be

And aren't we all divine?
Aren't we all running in time?
Watching life floating by
In a butterfly, a rhyme?

Aren't we all on the way back home?
Whether by boat, by train or by car
Don't we all crave our infinity?
Ever elusive, never far

Fade Away

Glover, Vermont

The human predicament
Is learning how to cope with death
We plant trees
We sing songs
We build bridges.

We try to do something
Build some legacy.

But we all fade away

We all fade away

Breathing

Lake Willoughby, Vermont

Everything is breathing
On top of everything else
That's breathing

We are all just pulling in,
And wading out.
Gently,
Endlessly

Me on the birch tree
The bug on my arm
The water on the rocks.
The sand
The hills
Breathing
Skin with different names
and patterns

Stretching
Adjusting to the sun
Tightening
Expanding

Laughter
Joy
Coming in
Going out
Back into itself

We breathe ourselves

In
and
Out

Stillness

Lake Willoughby, Vermont

What we are afraid of is
The stillness.

The stillness is so vast
That we don't know how to fit
Or what do do within it.

If we embrace the stillness enough
We cease
And are no longer.

Therefore, we cling to the changing.
The ups and the downs
Because the middle is still
Untrammeled
Like fresh snow
Forever and ever
With nowhere to go.

Nowhere to tread,
Nowhere to hide

So we crave something
That can take us outside of this calm
We like the stillness temporarily
But not for too long

For eternity
Is quite a long, long time.

And all that is there is stillness,
Never leaving
Never changing
Stillness.

Squinting at Death

Mount Moosilauke, New Hampshire

We squint at death
Like when we hit a dragonfly on the road while we're driving
Yet this squinting at death makes us shy away from life
It makes us question the divine timing of it all
Because we are always afraid our time to go will come sooner than it is supposed to
Yet we have no idea
We assume that by being careful
We stay safe
And so we domesticate ourselves
And we lose our wilderness
We lose our balance

The more we are afraid of death
The less we live into love

The more we cling to safety
The less we experience true freedom

What would life be anyway without the imminent risk of death?
Perhaps we can smile at death
And in turn, we begin to live our life
Untethered to our concerns of this world being the only one we'll ever know

Tree
Greenfield, MA

When you look at me
What do you see?

You're so much older than I
And wiser than me

With more humility
Standing, strongly rooted
Despite the howling winds

Giving everything
Expecting nothing

You feed us air
We chop you down
Make you into fiat
To chop you down some more
& plant mono crop poison.

How are you so kind,
So fecund
So gentle?

Housing beings
Big and small
Feeding all of them,
Intelligent and less intelligent
With nothing but a smile on your bark.

The ark
Was built of you
An escape route from the perils

You render yourself

Of service
And divide yourself up
To be used for the delivery of spirit
To higher ground.
For life.

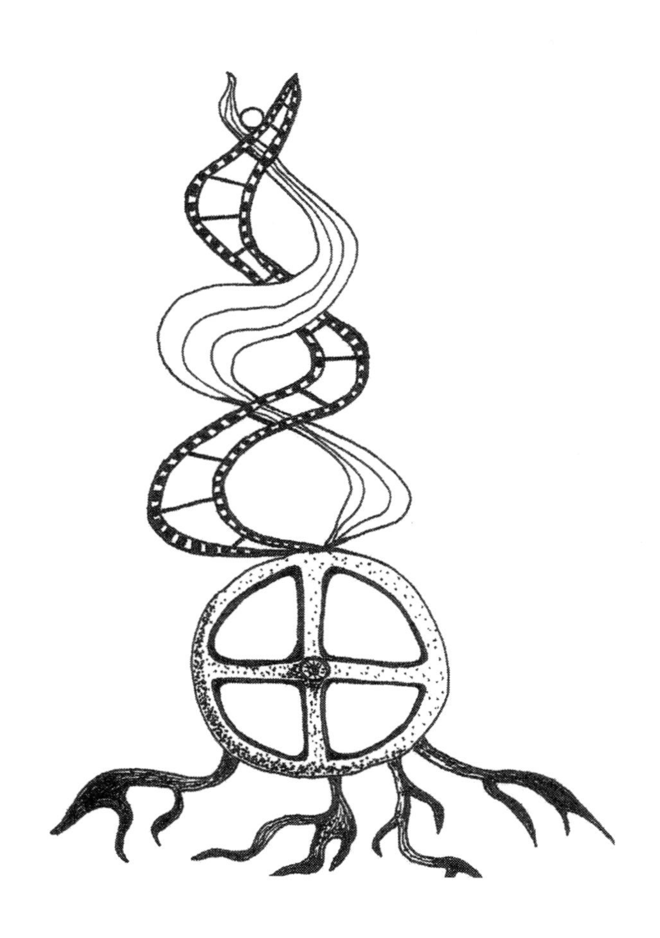

Choose

Greenfield, MA

Your instability is torturous;
You waver like a sapling in a westerly wind.
Your stability is admirable.;
Rooted firm in your mind soil like a sequoia tree.
But they contradict each other, so.
How can you say one thing,
Or even five things,
Yet when we lay together,
You reflect another wholly different world?
Within both lies the pearl.

You aspire for one-ness,
Yet live in a boundary filled world.
Who better to walk with you through the veil than me?
Apocalypse is but a jolting of the curtain,
Of moments eclipsed in their unfolding.

Insecurities emerge in your questioning,
Yet you are secure of your position in my eyes.
Why the anxiety?
I told you where I stand —
Either you're there whole-heartedly
Or not at all.
Like a statue begging the sands of time to slow,
Or a ghost of the summer leaves on the deadened tree branches of winter.

The choice is yours!
I am but a glimpse of life —
Coloured garments in a Moroccan bazaar,
And scented plumes of dream smoke puffed from a hookah in Mogadishu.

You can enter this film reel where the projectionist sits, torching cigarette burns in the top right corner like black bubbles of sun-soaked vision.

If not,
The film keeps rolling;
The holy director is building a masterpiece.

Ojai

Ojai, California

Fire,
Burn fire.
If you had five minutes
To choose what to bring
What would you leave behind?
To what would you cling?
Running away
From your own mistakes
What to leave in the past?
What futures you take?
Valley of Thunder
Strike of Lightning
Nature is strong
It's power, frightening

We are the rumble
We are the flash
Don't fear your own strength
Embrace the crash
Fire destroys the surface
But feeds the Earth
Creating the new
Time for rebirth

Palm Moon

Santa Barbara, California

Good evening, Palm moon
Happy to see you, tonight
In all your glory

Crescent like a smile
Face hidden in the dusk sky
Eyes watching us all

You pull the ocean
Coyotes howl for you
I'm a lunatic

A marker in time
Waxing and waning in rhyme
With our rocking tilt

Pocked by the cosmos
Not ashamed of your own scars
Shining in the dark

Receive the key

Buffalo, NY

We always ask questions to other people
Hoping that the will give us the key
To unlock something within us

Yet we are the key
And we are the lock
No one else can hand you a key!

The other is just a locksmith
You hand them your metals
You hand them your saw

And they craft and they carve
So the exact pattern of that key that you seek,
The one you have inquired about
Returns back to unlock yourself.

Love Yourself (An Ode to Black Rock City)

Andover, MA

Love yourself deeply
Like an unwavering flame
With infinite wick

The Earth loves herself
Through flowers and trees and birds
In commune they dance

And through her self love
She can love other beings
Unconditional

Not without this love
Deeper than the dark ocean
Can one share this field

Nor it diminish
From the act of the giving
It's source bountiful

Comprehension fails
To fathom the source of it
Pure humility

Strike your own matchstick
On the flint of gratitude
For you hold the breath

And in that inhale
Share in the blessing of life
Immemorial

We can show honor

By learning to love ourselves
Like plants love the Sun

Turning towards the light
That graces us with its rays
Even when it's dark

The Rope

St. Louis, Missouri

Sometimes when we are so deep in the well
And the sides slide up like infinite time
It becomes difficult to believe we will ever escape
That we can ever return again to the light
A tool we can use
Is a rope
The rope is our gateway out of the well
It's sinews fibrous and strong
It's grip, perfectly ergonomically engineered
The rope is our connection to something larger

A vantage point of vastness
Where we often forget
And by forgetting, we can remember
For only in acceptance of ignorance
Can there be wisdom
For only in deep fear
Can there be love
And instead of losing sight of the light
We accept that it never shall go astray
It never leaves the well
Only our attention is what must be brought back into focus
Until there is no more focusing
And no more well

Winter Porch

Andover, MA

The squirrel gathers his stance
After every jump
As the piano keys are played.
I gather myself,
As I sit in a winter jacket
Out on the open air porch,
Drinking Commanderie de la Bargemone
By myself.

Echoes of childhood,
Echoes of another world.
How strange to be in a place
But not of it.

A bird creaks in the chimney.
Exhaust fumes linger in the air behind cars
That scoot by on the frozen bitumen.
People step out of their house
To step back into their cars.
They step back out of their cars for a second
And back into a building.
Everyone's always going inside here
And not out.
Seems the opposite of their seeking.

Christmas around the corner,
Society obliging you to spend money
To show your Love.
I oblige.
I look to put down some of my righteousness
And meet people where they're at.
It's not easy.

Nine hours of sunlight a day

Don't do a body good,
Hard to be light bodied
With no sunlight.

New born day,
All I want to do is play,
But all I can do is lay.
Incubate these thought-eggs
So one day they may
Hatch.

Morphic Resonance

Salem, MA (at Jury Duty)

A crystalline
Morphic dream
Fluidity ain't what it seems.
Inverse states of form and energy
Forming endlessly
Towards organization.
Is it intergenerational mobility
That changes our formed state?
Navigating towards complexity
Or simplicity?
Is ascension just stability?
To achieve the crystal body
There must be regularity
And order.
But traditional thermodynamics
Limits our entropy,
Potentially.
Energy conservation is key,
We recover this through resonant memory,
Instead of variance
We find lack of change.
It may seem strange
For our fields to grow yieldlessly
But it depends on your metric
Of yield.
The probability
Says the Schrödinger in me,
Inlays patterns that splatter me spatially,
Matter of fact
I think my temporal's on track,
Temporarily.
Mechanistically,
The trick should be
Contemplation of the grand mystery—

As kids do see,
The vitality
That lies in habitual morality.
Instinctually,
In infancy,
Frailty will navigate beyond the seas,
With no memo to read,
No onboarding to feed,
Just perfectly designed embryonic seeds.
Epigenetically derived discovery.
We are the true explorers of infinity.

Chapter 3: Asia

There were a few different years that these poems were written. I believe the majority were in 2017 and late 2019/early 2020. The one from Thailand and from Bali maybe from 2015 if my memory serves me correctly.

Most of the poems are from India and Nepal; two of my favorite countries that I have traveled within thus far in my life. The majesty of the landscapes, the kindness of the people, the delicious sights, smells, tastes and sounds. All of it is pure magic.

In 2017 I spent about 6 weeks in India, starting in Uttarakhand and journeying through Rajasthan over to the Pakistani border as a part of a music festival called Kabir Yatra. This was quite an amazing experience, as musicians from all over India, from traditional Rajasthani musicians with mustaches to the twirling Bauls of Bengal, to popular singers from Mumbai came and spread the messages of the ecstatic poet Kabir on the partition line where the British divided India in accordance with the religions tensions at the time. The messages of Kabir are all about Love and to travel along this border was incredible.

After this music festival where we were all sleeping on floor mats in old school yards and outside on basketball courts, I journeyed from the border of Pakistan on a very long train ride across the country to Varanasi, and then attempted to get into Nepal via a legal border crossing at Raxaul. This did not happen because the train from Varanasi stopped in the middle of the night in the middle of Bihar with no more service to any border crossing station. This resulted in me hopping into a jeep stuffed with Nepali people looking to get back to their country, getting driven through Bihar at 4AM. The car so crowded that the stick shift was between my legs and two women in the seat behind me were asleep on my shoulders. Once we got to the border town, I was accidentally snuck across the border somewhere near Bairgania without a visa because that border was not able to give any foreigners a visa. This had to be ameliorated days later at the immigration office in Kathmandu which was a close call. All of this was mere days before I was supposed to start a month long Mahayana Buddhist meditation retreat at the well known Kopan Monastery in Kathmandu. After the retreat, I then went trekking in the Annapurna Reserve for a few weeks before heading to Australia for Christmas.

In late 2019 and early 2020 I ventured to Asia again, first stopping in Taiwan and then to Vietnam for a month before embarking to southern India for 3 months. This time in India, first in Mysuru, Karnataka and then down to Kerala was some of the most profound times of my life. It began with a 200 hour YTT in traditional Ashtanga Yoga at Yoga Gita with the teacher Sri. Vijay Gopala and ended learning Ayurvedic knowledge at a clinic and school in Kerala.

Bon voyage!

On the Inside Looking Out

Kopan Monastery, Kathmandu, Nepal

Down the hill and over the barbed wire,
And out into the city.
The Kathmandu valley,
Sprawling out below.
Music, haze,
Colorful buildings stacked on one another like Legos,
Trees.

I am feeling separate from this outside,
High up within the monastery gates,
Away from most of the noise and chaos.
But,
Not from the internal chaos.

We are all on the inside looking out,
Searching for respite from the chaos of uncontrolled thought streams
And desires.

Happiness and usefulness,
That's what the Dalai Lama said the purpose of life was;
Happy and useful.

How does one become happy?
What is useful?
Happiness can be from dedicating yourself
To the plight of all sentient beings,
Withdrawing from the external world,
And coming in.

Coming home.

Like leaving Kathmandu and coming up here.
Up the potholed hills of dust swirls,
Away from the side alleys filled with hustle and movement.

I've already thought about leaving here,
This peaceful land of fat rabbits and swooning pigeons.
Trickling fountains and flowers in bloom.
Is compassion an addiction?

Maybe I'll go trekking and get back into the action,
Since I think I will miss the perfect time to go.
Doubts.
It will be too cold, to snowy at the base camp,
Blah, blah, blah.

Am I cheating and not having gratitude?
Is everything I am seeking,
The fulfillment and the adrenaline
Already inside of me here inside these gates,
Inside of 'my' mind?

Karma ripened to bring me here, now,
In this place to learn with these people.
But there is much dogma as well,
Structured belief systems that still feels like religion.

What was I expecting?
All of these expectations!
Instant gratification expectations.
The curse of anticipation is when it doesn't happen.
So why expect anything at all?

Pure experiential reality is cutting through
All of these illusions,
Lifting the veil and exposing the things normally
Not directly exposed to the light.

Perhaps it is structured this way for people to
Grasp it on a large scale.
All I could think of when people stand and prostrate themselves
In front of the monastic teacher, not the Lama,

Is Terrence McKenna saying,
"Slamming your head against the ground or kissing someone's feet
Is not going to get you enlightened. It's all experiential."

On the inside looking out,
At all of the people here,
Going from monastery to monastery.
Tushita, Bodhgaya, Kopan.
Here, there,
Where is it all but in the mind?
When the reality is a dream,
And all of it isn't as it seems.
Is there an ultimate reality?
Why couldn't I not move from my seat in Massachusetts,
And learn with out access to these teachings through the
Akashic records?

Even Buddha learned from Indian gurus,
But were the gurus really aspects of his highest dimensional self?
Are we prostrating to our potentiality?
His innate wisdom, is our innate wisdom,
Which is the same wisdom of the One and all?
We are it.

Internal War

Hanoi, Vietnam

And the people sit in chairs
Blankly, outwardly they stare
Climbing stairs within their minds
As mindless music blares to pass the time

And the undetonated bombs they idly sit
From the USA's geo-political whip
Internally builds the rage
A military-industrial complex cage

Exhaust chokes out the sky
Buildings keep climbing high and high
The people can't say why
The reason hidden on the other side

But the noodle pots still steam
And the eyes, they still gleam
With a hope beyond the fear
That something approaches near

Whether it be freedom from suffering
Attained from wealth
Or blessings from health
Nay, avoidance from the stealth
Of capitalists' creeping mouth

Consuming as it makes others do
Like pho
Slurping up the land it has in sight
Two wrongs don't make a right
But I find this internal fight
Between giving up
And stoking the life

Inside my fire to change
Continuously amongst the complacent
As they sit and watch adjacent
And the world slowly burns without a mention
The path to hell paved with these good intentions

But inaction leaves me stuck
With the others who glamorously give no fucks
And take selfies and scarf the life
That causes all the strife
Words as empty as a flask
On a drunken bastard's ass
After a night out on the town
Vomit splattered on the ground

Then the sun rises again
And he crawls into bed away from that light
Of an old, old friend
Swept into the sewer the spittle goes
Rats munching in the undertow
My ego flares up like smoke
Off a plastic fire
Fumes gagging me
As I try to prevent this landfill.

If I harm myself in the process
Is that progress?

Or am I just permanently depressed
Density coming in
As I shift from realm to realm
Protect me please from this
The bright light with equal darkness
In its midst

Nepali Boddhisattva

Annapurna Conservation, Nepal

If I could I'd put shoes on all the porter's feet,
So they didn't have to drag goods up the mountain in sandals.
If I could I'd shine a light on everybody I meet,
To remind them that inside of them, there shines a candle.

If I could I'd clean all the air from the Kathmandu streets,
So the Newar people didn't have to cough in the smog.
If I could I'd show people that all beings were our mothers,
So they wouldn't kill the chickens or kick the stray dogs.

& for all of this I'd ask nothing,
Compassionately detached action,
No reciprocity needed, no thoughts of receiving anything.
The Bodhisattva treads acting as the moment calls for,
And once the action is done, their feet hit the floor.

If I could I would teach everyone to stop using plastic,
And that Gaia is a living organism and not a trash bin.
If I could I would unfold the veil of fear and greed,
And show that competition is another form of sin.

If I could I'd show people the beauty in front of their eyes,
And that they don't need to wait until death to experience Heaven.
If I could I would eliminate all needs to lie,
Because acting in truth and integrity opens up the sacred seven.

& on this path of giving, the bodhisattva walks alone,
Where beings are suffering is where he calls his home,
Drifting like a tumbleweed out across song lines,
Working within reality, shape-shifting in time.

Being a part in this world but not truly of it,
Relaxed half-gaze, inter-dimensional sight.
Real eyes realize the extraordinariness of this life.
A peace walker, truth talker, guardian of the Light.

The Fan

Rishikesh, India

The dogs were barking for about an hour
Before I decided to turn on the fan.

It's rhythm,
Constant.
It's rotation,
Predictable.

Why does this predictability
And constancy
Help us
To fall asleep?
Is it the fact our minds
Have something else to focus on
Other than what's happening directly
Around us?

Is it us knowing what is to come
In the fans planned rotation and whirr
That allows us to finally relax?
Is it something about the circular pattern
That hypnotizes us
Into a doze?

For the fan could surely fly off its hinges!
Decapitating us,
Shattering the windows
And breaking the bathroom door.

But,
That's an outlier...Right?
The fan is at first,
A mechanism
For keeping us cool,

Warding off the summer heat
When we feel it the most.
Protecting us
From the elements
Of nature.
If only for some time
It helps to make us
Content in our surroundings.

These elements of the natural world
Are wild,
Unpredictable
And not always to our liking.
Sometimes they may even make you sweat
Or make your heartbeat
Faster than normal.
The heat and humidity of the night,
Or a slight sound in the bushes,
Or a falling rock.

So what is the fan really
But a symbol of
Comfort?
A symbol of routine?
Our Cyclical nature,
In Samsara.

Should I shut it off?

The Subtleties

Jodphur, Rajasthan, India

It's the subtleties I like.
Not the big forts on the hill,
That summon and demand attention,
Democratizing violence and war;
Like a vacuum sucking your eyes upward.

I enjoy the living quarters,
Breathing,
Pulsing,
The Heartbeat of a city.
The decrepit blue gated door,
With crumbling white stone pillars,
Rusting metal,
And exposed red brick underneath.

The small candle,
With no more wick,
Burnt out in ceremony,
Evidenced by the blackened spot marks,
Around the enclave where its flame once wavered.

The dog on the street,
Kicking its back feet,
Sniffing the air.
Not finding much but pollution
From a passing motorcycle,
As he ducks out of the way
And into a a nap
After the trash pile looking for food,
came up empty.

The woman in the the pink sari,
Carrying a baby fern in a pot
Towards her house,

Which is most likely tucked back in
One of these winding, small alleyways,
That are so easy to get lost in.

The cows,
Smiling in a circle.
Eyes closed
Soaking up the sun,
Underneath ancient blue buildings,
Without a care in the world
Because they are sacred here.

The bicycle
With shiny ruffles still hanging
From the Diwali celebration that just passed.
Yet, still gathering heaps of dust
And rust,
And holes in the seat,
And pigeon poop splattered
On its rims.

The gold daggers
Hanging in the clock shop,
With rubies in the handles,
Guarded by a mustached man,
Who looks tired,
But patient in the
Constant beeping street chaos
That zooms by him everyday.

It's the chai man,
Sitting under a huge Bodhi tree
Who's feet are like the Earth.
Who waves you off to not pay
Every time you visit his chai stand,
Even though you want to.
The guest is God here,

Even if the host is too.

These are the things I like.
They don't demand your attention,
And may not get notoriety,
But they deserve it.
They are the true respiration,
& circulation,
Pumping blood and sensation
Throughout the capillaries
Of a place in time.

Vagabonders

Ubud, Bali

Fellow Vagabonders, young and old
Listen close to the great stories told!
Told by the road, the trees and the lake,
Keep your senses keen to truth and have a sense for the fake.
Sniff up the smells and taste the great feasts,
Revel in small victories and acknowledge defeats.
As opportunities flip and get turned on their head,
Cherish a warm shower and a nice comfy bed.
Gaze into the eyes of your brothers and sisters,
Reconnecting with their souls, for our journeys are twisters.
Spiraling together in interwoven intricacies,
Adding to the beauty and never-ending mystery.
Alas! Freedom and sovereignty the goal,
Travel holistically, aimed for the whole.
A holy lust for life, absorb and remember,
Forget and forgive, and egos, dismember
Love and love and love and love,
It's all we need to be at peace and not to shove.
We are it,
We are infinite.

The Greatest Engineer

Koh Lanta, Thailand

God, you're the greatest engineer
It's amazing to see
All the cliffs and the rocks and the birds and the trees
Your hand carves the most exquisite and beautiful art I've ever seen.

So diverse and so colorful
All we can do is hope to imitate
The wonder and splendor of your creation
So original and free
All we can do is hope to become that vibration.

From the caves of the Phi Phi islands
To the black fish in waterfalls of Litchfield
There is infinite magnificence
In what you do yield

All perfectly in tune
Perfectly in sync
Perfectly working together
Symbiotically linked

God you're the greatest engineer
And I'm loving this life so much!
And that's just nature, and we humans get to touch.
Get to feel and smell and taste and see
The miracles that have been placed all around us by thee

The smell of eucalyptus on a warm summers night
The last rays of sun dipping below the ocean and out of sight
The feel of your loved one's Heart beating against your own
The longing for family, and a home away from home

These physical vehicles perfectly engineered to deliver these spirits
Holding the soul in the wind, we can hear it

Enabling us all the tools we need to fulfil our purpose here
To learn, to grown, to give back, to not fear

To live in the love that is eternal in your kingdom and home
To have a peasants eyes but a seat on the throne
Please help me to keep learning and growing every day
Please help me to be a flute for the sweet music you play

Please help me to walk in blessing wherever I go
And please help me to spread that same blessing once I hit the road
Please help opportunity and abundance abound
Please help me interpret the truth from the sound

I'm sorry for anyone I've hurt in my life
Through words, actions, thoughts or conduct, it cuts like a knife
I forgive those who have doubted or made fun of me
I forgive those who judged because they did not see how or what I see

Thank you for the blessings bestowed upon I
Thank you for your creation, thank you for the sky
Thank you for the rain and the sun and the flowers
Thank you for everything, I am grateful for your power
Every hour, every minute
Every second that we're in it

Sanctuary Amidst the Chaos

Jiufen, Taiwan

How do we allow our beings to function as a constant haven
When the current world-view is so abrasive and insensitive to most things,
Yet overly sensitive to others?

Being here reminds me that we have so, so far to go
With reforming the day-to-day activities of our lives
And to look beyond the minutia
That is dwelled upon
And to meet at the field beyond it.

Field as a grassy knoll,
Or field as an energetic field,
A dimension,
A frequency.

The amount of plastic used here in one day is horrifying,
and not one person bats an eye.
Yet, some of the bathrooms are gender neutral, and if not, an uproar!

Can there be a balance, perhaps?
A lantern-focus instead of a spotlight?
The more light, the more darkness, that's duality.
What are we focusing on?
More and more division arises from more and more segmentation of that focus.

Man's war against nature.
Wilderness is the enemy
Because of its inability to be controlled
Which leads to our own surrender and recognition of the fact
That we are not in control.
Nature is so humble,
Continually giving and asking only to be cared for in return,
To be tended.

When it is tended, it's a closed loop.
No need to consume beyond our measures,
No need to continually be caught in the mind,
We are grounded, literally.
Ever wonder why it's so hard to be grounded in a city?
Where's the ground?

Nothing is sustainable beyond the community threshold level,
That is why prior to the rapid spread of this exploitative OS
There was such understanding and abundance with our natural ecosystems.
It was rooted in reality,
Not illusion.

All I can see while here in Taiwan
Are the pigs from the Miyazaki film 'Spirited Away',
Wondering,
If it's all a reflection,
Am I this too?
Where has my unconscious greed led me?
I guess to this tea house
Where these thoughts come through to be shared with you.
Take what you will,
And plant the rest.

The Doorman

Bus from Pokhara to Kathmandu

There're places to be gone
And the bus is leaving now
Are you on it or not?
Kathmandu! KatmanKatman Kathmandu!
Yes or no?
Hop off, slap the bus when yer on
And keep it moving.

Feel the wind in my hair
Hang out the bus door
Fingers gripping the hinges
Spit some taback &
Take a look back to make sure I didn't miss any potential customer.

Get people on,
Count the money
Make sure the bus riders are in line,
Playing Tetris with humans and the seats
Bags of rice and potatoes
Stacked like bricks.

I'm happy if you're happy.
That's the job of the doorman.
But the dream and rush of the doorman
Extends beyond the economics.

It's a sense of freedom,
Constant vantage point
A foot in two worlds,
The inner and the outer.
The inner of warmth and relative safety,
The outer, harsh;
Mixed with exhaust smoke and
Cool breezes,

As the bus hurtles down treacherous
Potholed roads.

Kathmandu! Kathmandu! Katmankatmankatmandhu!
Keep the grip strong
And my stance sturdy,
Or else I'm toppling overboard.
Peep a young buck
Slapping the back of the bus
Guiding it's blind reversal
Onto the trafficked road.
He sprints around the bus when it's guided safety,
And gives the older door man
The eyebrow nod;
The doorman salute.

From one doorman to another,
A young buck to a bus elder,
One eager for the ropes and one
Who has been on them for a while,
A quick smile,
And we're off again.

World in my Bones
Annapurna Conservation, Nepal

I've got the world in my bones
From traveling around,
Be it the mountains in the sky
Or the plants in the ground.

I got the world in my body,
From all these years of drifting.
Cutting strings to the world,
Becoming permanently lifted

Gifted in my speech,
Infinite in my reach
All I need to do is
Manifest without a preach.

Ambition is the slave master
But I am not a slave
The most important thing for life
Is the recognition of the grave.

Death is certain
But the time is unknown
Why waste your time
Running from your own home?

Run back to the soul
The one that's beginning less
The most supreme in this world
The one that we all miss

When we stray far away
Distance in the heart
Feels like canyons
Pulling us apart.

No King, Happy Journey

Thiruvananthapuram, Kerala, India

No king
Happy journey
Happy journey
The long winding road of education
Which is self-study
No teacher
No student
You're on your own
Following guideposts along the way
Knowledge is just information
Wisdom cannot come from it
Experience is the only source of this treasure
And it is not a secret how to find it
You just stop looking outward
And look within
No king
Happy journey
Happy journey
The Yatra back
To the Heart
Where to start?
On the trains through trash infernos
Dead dogs and burnt logs
Deep depths of the dark nights of the ego
That bring the soft morning sunlight to who you imagine you are
Showing you as dawn dissipates
that you're not even that
As you're just a medium for the light to catch on to
Passing by like suns rays on rainy days
The moments of measuring our true Self is in the moments between actions
In the waiting
The stillness that is the only entrance point into the portal of experience
Without that quiet
That silence

That alone-ness
You can experience nothing
Only fragmented chunks of thought
Which you try to weave together and label as a story of continuity
Utilizing a limited point of view
Trapped in your time-space locus
This ain't no hocus pocus
The duality only exists when there is a You!
Without you
There is an essence
And everything is the same
Pleasure turns to joy
And joy is the celebratory dance of Life
Nataraja in Ananda Tandava
As it all falls away
This psychological death is the true rebirth
Into the vastness of Bliss
No king
Happy journey
Happy journey

Don't Blame the Mirror

Elathoor, Kerala, India

If you see your face
And it looks quite ugly to you
Do you throw away the mirror?
Do you blame the reflection?
If you see a king
As angry, gross and gluttonous as can be
Do you bow to him
And give him your praises
Like the rest of the flock?
Or do you remain standing
And risk being pelted by the judgements of others?
When a dog barks
At a child molester
But you don't know what he is
Do you blame the dog
And tell it to stop barking,
While saying "sorry sir"
As he walks to the playground?
I hope you never blame the mirror
Or praise that horrible king
Or get upset at the dog
The reflection itself is not the culprit.
One must gaze at oneself,
Really, look!
From a cleansed eye
Unclouded by the cataracts of conditioning,
To see what's Truly happening.
The happening is
Beyond your theatrical mind games,
Looking to sell out its tickets to the show
To your own critics and fans

Wherever I am, There I am

Wayanad, Kerala, India

We atop the rock
In God's country we go roam
Our Soul is our home

We never alone
No matter how far we stray
We can never leave

All the world we walk
Looking out of the same eyes
That slowly can see

Wherever I am
I'm there all over again
We have never left

Nothing there to do
Nothing to try or to find
It is all inside

The outside is there
An exploration platform
To find us unwound

Stillness in the sound
Effortless standing on ground
Until the light comes.

Rubies and Gold

Aluva, Kerala, India

I collect rubies and gold
Out of the dumpsters
What else to do
When all of the worlds treasures
Are treated as trash?
Street urchins poke out of alleys
While mussels get popped like muscles
Reflected in chandeliered ceiling mirror tiles
In rooms as flat as irons
I peer in the windows
No ones there
I peer in their houses
No ones home
Rusted signs swing crusted over in dust
Collecting busted up lack luster paint chips sealing
the zippered in Holocene
With a hermetically sealed ego-gleam
I peer in the offices
Everyone's working
On what?
I am not sure
Spiritual fashion
Contraception delivery
New toys for puppies
More ways to get more energy for cheap
Some new sustainable shoe lace
No matter how much energy is generated
The energy drains out of porous sponge brains quicker than it can be created
As vampiric programs spew moronic neuroses overloaded
to those in states of comatose
United by patriotism
Divided by the same coin
Right on the opposite side
Like we forgot it had two tides

High and low
We move so fast but evolve so slow
Crawling and sprawling and falling again and again
Reaching out for hands of friends
Yet they turn out to be merely men
The end
Can never exist without a beginning
Destruction
Means creation
Look on the streets
See who you meet
They may have stories of glory to tell about well, all of their Heavens and
Hells that simultaneous
Simon never says he just tells
If you're always hiding and we never seek
If you always act strong you truly are weak
If you're always talking then you never really speak
Noise is coming out but I don't hear a peep
Back out to the treasure troves Long forgotten I creep
Slipping into the eternal dream
As I awake from my sleep

Chapter 4: Australia

I lived in Australia on and off from about 2015 to 2017, mostly in Western Australia. My partner lived in different parts of Perth and I lived with her, sometimes working random jobs or sometimes just enjoying the Australian beach-life. I didn't really write much in these times. I'm not exactly sure what I was doing, actually.

All but one of the poems were written in Western Australia. One of them was written in the Northern Territory near Darwin, where we also traveled and lived briefly in 2015.

Many of these poems were pertaining to dreams. When down camping in the Karri forests near Boranup were some of the places where the imagery was the strongest. I felt very peaceful there.

Snakes were a common theme of my dreams while in Australia. Later after these dreams came to a cessation, after meeting an elder of the Larrakia people in Darwin, she shared with me briefly some Aboriginal belief systems after the fact helped me connect this realization to perhaps a connection with the Rainbow Serpent. Rainbow Serpent dreaming is a strong force and image in many different Australian Aboriginal groups and is related to water and rain.

Australia is a place that felt extremely ancient while I was there. The deserts, the rivers, the trees, the animal life. Whenever I landed in Perth, I always remember the warm evening night air and driving through the back roads smelling Eucalyptus, Peppermint Trees and Melaleuca. It is quite a beautiful, diverse and powerful continent and I miss it dearly.

A Lone Tree is Never Lonely

Margaret River, Western Australia

A lone tree,
Sits in a rancher's field.
Wind swept
So it has a tilt
Away from the Ocean.

Not even the cows lay under it.
Crows balk at it,
Rarely standing on it's warped limbs.

Yet, it stands strong and alone.

Fenced in,
Away from the public's eye and mind,
Except for those who feel it calling for them.
Those who want to climb it, hug it.
Thank it for being unique,
And providing us with oxygen to breathe,
And inspiration to perceive.

Weathered in time by the elements,
Unrelenting,
Since it's birth as a young treeling,
Tree-king.
Sprouted alone away from the grove
Of beautiful Karri trees down the road.
A seed picked and dropped from passing avian life.

The grove dwellers all have each other to keep company,
Roots interconnected to communicate through,
& creaking whispers to giggle at when the wind exhales.

These grove trees never experience aloneness,
But, perhaps they experience loneliness,

Sitting idly amongst the collective-mind and companionship.

Not the lone tree,
Who sits calm,
Observing the world solitarily,
From its open field of possibilities.
It doesn't require anything for it
To be completely at peace with its aloneness.
Alone, but connected to
It all.

Ocean

Conto's Beach, Margaret River, Western Australia

Gaia's waves,
Are her communication system.

Slowly rolling in as the
Wind blows,
Sun sets
&
Moon rises.

So clear and flat is the horizon,
That you see the peaks of infinite waves,
Far off in the distance,
Rolling in with messages.

Crashing.
Caressing the rocks in frothing white foam.
Hugging them in ecstatic sensuality after the passing of time
Since they were last in embrace.
Feeling into the sensors of the rocks themselves,
Delivering intelligence
From shores far away.
This intelligence is shared with this shore
That I'm sitting on now,
And all inhabitants of it.

I can feel it.

Simultaneously, the waves receive information
From this shore's neural network of
Shrub bush, sand crystals,
Magpie calls, Kangaroo Paw roots
& various flower scents.

It is all gathered,

Then reverberated back off of the resonant field
That the land holds at this moment in time.
Has there been a stressor? A fire?
A storm? Is it too dry for thriving life?
Was there a harmful act against life here?
A malign intent?

All of it is felt,
Connected and communicated,
Bounced back through the waves in slow motion,
As they withdraw their silky hold with the rocks.
Bidding them adieu,
As they slip back into the ocean for their long journey back.

Rolling,
Returning to that which it was and always has been.
Merely changing directions,
With a new story to tell.

Snake

Cottesloe, Perth, Western Australia

Shedding layers of skin,
Moving on without looking back,
On their layers left behind.
These layers no longer serve them,
So what's to dwell on?

Low to the ground,
Slithering through sand seeking shade,
Leaving nothing behind but a small line,
From their non-linear bodily path.

Snakes get a bad rap,
The fall of humanity and all that.

Poison and protection,
Knowledge and truth,
Simplicity in structure and form,
Flexible and cunning,
Malleable and quick,
Decisive and discerning.

Saw one at the trail to Conto's.
Greenish brown tail whipped across the walking path,
As it zoomed into the bush.
Meter, meter and a half probably.

Life isn't about accumulating layers or ornaments and depth,
It is about shedding them.

To the true essence
That moves you in that moment, that season,
For smooth motion and (e)motion,
Barely being noticed.

The Ouroboros is a snake that eats its own tail,
Symbolizing the cyclical nature of things
& the supreme mystery
Of life needing to consume itself to survive.
Day in and day out,
Everything is eating everything;
Consuming.
Yet, this snake,
This representation of life,
When it does consume itself,
As when we consume our own ego,
Enter into the Oneness of things.
Not looted or polluted by
Self-deception
Or our mind's conception of what is possible.

Not limited,
But liberated by the impossible.

Too Many

Wandi, Western Australia

Too many chemists, not enough chemistry
Too many socialites with anti-social tendencies
Too many strangers who glance at you like enemies
Too many panaceas and not enough small remedies

Way too many children with way too much technology
Way too many people fronting skipping out on honesty
Way too many false prophets preaching tabloid prophecy
Exceptions to a rule being punished and labeled oddities

Far too many polygamists trying out monogamy
Far too many humans with no idea of geography
Cultures folded sideways 'til they're just a boxed origami
Far too many monsters proliferating this monstrosity

Way too few people who don't even know their neighbors name
Way too few people accepting responsibility instead of diverting blame
Way too few who know that there is no reason for shame
Way to few people who know that life is not a waiting game

Too little effort and fun put in preparing our own food
Too little effort to protect the homeless who are kicked and shooed
Too little effort giving back to those who have been purposely exploited and screwed
Too little people glued to nature instead of glued to the tube

When things come up and you're looking down please walk out to the jungle
Give me a ring I'll be swaying like the little king's bungalow
By the sea or in a tree or in the Bungle Bungles
Learning to be calm and quiet and learning to be humble.

Crocodile Energy

Mount Magnet, Western Australia

In the deep green waters where the crocodiles dwell,
Lives a man underneath the surface.
And he sprinkles sands of time over red rock cliffs of rhyme,
And puts the pieces of the species back in line.

This man's been here for a long, long time
Times before the clock, times before the rocks,
And times before the chicken or the egg.
This man is just a soul in a vehicle of old,
Morphing and shape shifting with the winds.

And as the winds have blown in dust
And the signs all turn to rust
This man waits for those to come to him.
So he can send his message out, with a whisper not a shout
For those who have an ear and have a will.

A will to see the Truth and a will to be the way
Through the clutter and falsities of modern day
So come out to the gorge
Where the crocodiles lay
To see what this man inside of you has to say.

Silence is the New Loud

Rapid Creek, Northern Territory, Australia

Silence is the new loud
Alone is the new crowd
Kind is the new mean
Dirty is the new clean
Clever is the new funny
Experience the new money
Veggies are the new meat
Actions the new seat
Walking is the new plane
Humble is the new vain
Love is the new fear
Third eyes are the new ears
Bravery's the new scared
Flowing the new prepared
Clean water is the new wine
Community the new mine
Food is the new meds
Hearts are the new heads
Hugs are the new drugs
Solar is the new plug
Mystery's the new answer
Healthy is the new cancer
Balancing is the new Tao
Now is the new now!

What Is Missing?

Wandi, Australia

Missing someone or desiring certain dates in time,
Like a wedding or birthday
To wish the family was together or whatever,
Are, to me are absurd notions.
Why wait for some day to really honor the presence
And company of individuals in your life whom you love?

Why not make that day like any other ordinary day,
Each of which is extra ordinary!
I see the novelty of such, birth day and wedding and this and that,
But missing someone or any attachment emotion
Is as fleeting as one cloud in the sky blocking the Suns rays from splaying their light Across the branches of a Bottlebrush tree.

The ego seems to seek this control, this certainty.
But nothing can be certain as long as our each and every breath
Is a gift given to us from some omnipresent creative force
That has allowed us to experience this blessing called life
In a perfectly engineered vessel
To deliver the spirits witnesses of its own blessing of which it sprung.

We cling to these moments, these paths, as identifiers.
Validation of some place we stand to feel grounded in something
That is illusory in itself.

Hierarchical by nature when that path makes one feel superior or inferior to another, giving away power instead of empowering others
Empathetically through compassionate action.
Even spending your life with someone like in a wedding.
Spend all your time with one person?
Investing everything you have into one being?
A business man would suggest you diversify your investment portfolio
Or a farmer would plant redundant crops to ensure that if one doesn't flourish than she or he can still eat and feed the family.

How can Love be limited to such?
It is unfair and cruel to project on a partner the ridiculous notion
Of being able to fulfill all terrestrial,
Spiritual
Physical
& metaphysical needs of one another
While juggling all personal development and joyous interactions with life
In all its levity and colors and Is-ness.

Love is infinite!
And, like Knowledge,
No matter how much you give our or share
You can always give more
& you never run out.

It builds like a volcanic inferno
As we rise in Love instead of fall.

Eternal Springs blossom,
Which can be followed by the autumns shedding of old,
Mulching the trees and feeding roots
To prepare for more blossoms.
The seasonality of love and of life.

The Blame Game

Cottesloe, Western Australia

The blame game,
A finger pointed out is one in vain.
Who's afraid of the shame
Of accepting responsibility?

The blame game,
Expectation's names
Unfulfilled, so who's to blame,
For this different picture of now?

The blame game,
Internal reality manifests external same,
A candle with two wicks burns with one flame.
Soon the wax runs out.

The blame game,
Love and compassion maimed,
The mind must be tamed,
Or reason will escape.

The blame game,
The true-self must exclaim
To snuff ego's acclaim,
And transcend the whole show.

Chapter 5: Hawai'i

My favorite place on the planet. The place that I really feel like my life river shifted courses. I first went to Hawai'i in 2013, to the island of O'ahu. My visa for India had just been denied and I was looking for somewhere to go after I had just quit a job. I somehow landed with a volunteer farming job on an artist village run by a Sri Lankan yogi in Wai'anae, which is on the west-side. On this sacred island my eyes began to open up to more and more things that I could've ever imagined.

I continued to travel back to the islands for about 2-3 months at a time for the next seven years. Back to O'ahu and over to Maui, Kauai to Hawai'i (Big Island) these islands really felt like home. A home that I had never really known. The ocean, absolutely incredible and fierce yet purifying and gentle. Fruits and mountains and mist and rain and culture and everything. This is also where I first began working with the land, or as the Hawai'ians call it, the 'āina.

These poems were written sometime between 2013-early 2020, so the voice may be varied as a lot of change continued to happen over these seven years, and is still happening now.
I cannot even begin to imagine where I would be right now if I had not taken the so-called risky step and ventured out to the islands.

Only When: The Pearl

Na'alehu, Hawai'i

Only when my boat fully capsized in the waves
Could I see the pearl

Only when I could witness that the ills and woes of the world were my own
Could I become healthy and free

Only when everything had collapsed under the weight of my self-proclaimed identity
Could I begin to rebuild

Only when I was burnt by the fire that I started
Could I understand its power and ferocity
And that fire cannot burn itself

Only when everyone turned their backs on me and ignored me
Could I see that I had turned my back on myself

Only when the rains started to fall to wash me clean
Could I know I was crying from happiness and sadness
Simultaneously

Only when everything is taken away from me
Can I understand that I never had it anyway

Only when God stares in my face in the mirror and tells me the Truth
Can I shatter my own lies

Only when I realize that I am the most prolific writer of my own suffering
Can I resign from my authorship

Only when my heart beats so fast that it is going to break
Can I understand that I have been afraid my whole life of things that are not real

Only when my loved one's eyes are blank, blanketed in compassion and anguish
Can I see what it is to be torn in two by Love

Only when I sensed betrayal
Can I understand the extent of my own duplicity upon myself

Only when all alone in the world
Can I understand the difference between loneliness and being alone
And that I am the problem and the solution

Only when the wolf inside howls for the blood moon
Can I see how small I am in the scheme of the shifting tides of the cosmos
Pulled like a wave in the galactic vacuum of my own mind

Only when I scream from the depths of my Being
Can I see how long I have been mad at the master I have become to the slave I was

Only when I laugh after it all
Can I see what the divine play of Lila really is

Only in an empty kitchen, filled with things
Can I see how you can never be nourished by the emptiness of the material worlds

Only when I zoom out
Can I really zoom back in
And see that everything is the same, again and again
Stories relentlessly playing themselves out like a VHS machine

Only when I see that I am the jailor
The judge and the criminal
Can I dissolve the entire court system from its legal framework

Only when I've lost the home of my Heart
Can I return to it and skip alongside the river bend

to the sweet song of Remembrance
That I've forgotten in the vastness of my own fantasy
Only when
Only when

Lomi Lomi

Honolulu, O'ahu

Surrendering to the island's embrace
Is like lomi lomi.
Are you prepared for what you've asked for?
Can you receive the blessings if they come in a form you didn't expect?
Healing isn't always smooth,
Deep tissue ebb & flows,
Shifting out stagnation,
Opening up for penetration;
With a relaxed gaze.

How do non-linear minds focus
In the 3D holographic matrices?
Perhaps it is un-focusing,
Becoming One with the field itself,
Morphic resonances entering into our cellular biologies,
As we enhance our sensitivities
By allowing barriers to dissipate in the breeze.

Breathe it in,
Through cooperation in family hood,
Seems too easy to be misunderstood.
We over stand the gentle way,
When we give in and start to play.
Not child-ish but child-like,
Full of wonder and kindness,
Unconditional love in judgmental blindness.
Mahalo nui.

Who/What/When/Where/Why

Honolulu, O'ahu

Who chirps with the birds and swims with the whales
Weaving cultures together through mutual tales
Who has skin of one color but a Heart of them all
Can lead us together, holding hands, standing tall

What rises in love can never fall in return
Once you integrate experience you continue to learn
What path once was clear becomes the formless soul
Delicately intertwined to the indivisible whole

When the colors meld at the brink of dawn
The hunter admires the mother and fawn
When common good surpasses selfish intent
Ego's self deception sits and laments

Where intuition and intention meet
Wind merges with ground and touches your feet
Where changes give way to maturation
Love conquers all fear and trepidation

Why we've taken so long to summon this collective memory
Our human language has separated us into a you and me
Why we're remembering now is a mystery to I
An intelligent information download from the sky

Tide Pool

Pu ʻuhonua o Hōnaunau, Hawaiʻi

I rise to pass away
That is the only way

I fear to remember what Love is
It is what it is

I hurt to become joyous
Heaviness becomes buoyant

I live to share
Give your heart with care

Childhood Dreams

Fern Forest, Hawai'i

Childhood dreams
Manufactured by the culture we see
Just like missiles and m-16s
I wonder how we would dream
If the children could just run free
To where would their untethered passions lead?
Without any barrier in between
Who they are and who they should be
We're caught in the middle of a transition
Where I only see one mission, one vision
The elimination of division with a precision
Exacting a sharpened dagger-like incision
A lobotomy of societal conditions
That place us as the recipient of religion
Rather than the deity itself
Stripping us of all our intuition
In the name of rationale
Well, lookey here, pal
When the value system shifts from the accumulation to the condensation
And your rewarded for not what you have but rather the dispensation
Then there will be a humanitarian initiation into the realms of Dasoham
The merging pragmatically of an existential Truth that we are all now acknowledging with this planned pandemic
For only once we stop following the leader like the recess game
Can we reclaim our own leadership
For only once we see our own fear of responsibility which is why we rely on a centralized agent to manage us
can we stop diverting blame and responsibility onto other parties and reclaim our own sovereignty
Step by step
Deed by deed
We are what we bleed
We're the medicine we need
Cut the chord

Plant the placenta and the seed
Remove the roots of your greed
So that no more fruits of poison shall yield
From your garden, indeed
And once we've begun to unweave
All these years of being deceived
We can finally be relieved
Of our desire to be free

E Pele

Kīlauea Iki Crater, Hawai'i

E Pele
Burn lava burn
Burn out the impurities of my Heart
Burn out the impurities of my Mind
Please continue to show me the way
Show me there is no difference
Between where I end and you start
Your art, the transformational fire
Decoupling emotional penetration with escapism
As conflict is just an invitation to intimacy
The beast guards the core wound
Poke it and watch it scream!
Burn the walls within which we shackle ourselves
Burn the fog off of our cavernous identities
Compensatory from defending what need not be defended
We too, like this island are still forming
Unlearning, re-patterning
Ever new, every momentous moment
Start again
Mirror mirror on the wall, who's the fairest of them all?
Be fair to yourself
Be equanimous with your equanimity
Our longevity depends on our levity
Angels fly because they take themselves lightly
Our fluidity, adaptability and virility
But the foxes guile mildly beguiles our mildest sense of the vast wild hidden within our smiles
as we domesticate our un-tameable Self
underneath The shield of societal validation and personal stealth sabotage
A global-Self-collage
Burn away the division within my vision
Burn away the precision within my own righteousness
& let the lava stones fall where they may
Kapoho pools, Pavlov's drool

Gandhi's spool or Baby Ruth pool
Call yourself out on your own shit
Shack up to shack down
Deconstruct to come back to the ground
Level of your Soul
Construction is destruction
Destruction is birth
Birth is death
Death is breath
Burn our illusions of grandeur with your inferno of might
Illuminating orange the night
Burn this fright of 'me'
The Me which thinks that it will disappear
Which is the root of all fear
Down to the struts and the piers
Releasing me from this hold I have on myself
Which part of us needs to die but doesn't want to?
Burn it all
Burn it all
So the Ohia can sprout tall
Burn it all
No rise without the fall
Peace rests alone after all

Sunrise
Hualālai, Hawai'i

Everyone wakes up
To a new day everyday
The sun still rises

Lest we forget that
Each new moment is a day
And time, relative

Can we start again
Every moment of our lives
Like the morning sun?

If we can do so
Innocent and blossoming
We unfurl like spring

And allow process
To reign supreme over goal
A verb over noun

All of the posion
Is medicine in disguise
Just open your eyes

A shattered fragment
Reclaim your disavowed parts!
Become whole again

Clouds on a Plane

Honolulu, O'ahu

Slow down
Take a deep breath
Why are you rushing?
Everything will get done
In it's own time.

Why are we always trying to get it all done anyway?
Here, there
What about the in-between?
Amidst the unknown,
In it's own time.

Time,
Throwing a net on infinity.
Beginninglessness has no boundaries.
Black matter consciousness expanding
Just beyond our grasp.

If there's a solution, why worry?
If there's not a solution, why worry?

Smell a flower,
Watch it bloom.
Listen to your favorite tune.
Chew your food,
Really, chew it!
Horace Fletcher used to do it, too.

After you take that picture,
Look with your own camera lens,
And breathe in your environment.
The connection and inspiration must start internally,
Before you externalize them.

There's no rush,
Death comes when it does,
It's part of the whole, being born thing.

This precious human life,
Starts to zip by
Like clouds out of the window of a plane.

So, slow down!
Savor the sensations
Without the mind jumping to premature conclusions and labels.
Although we continue forever,
Each moment is a precious gift,
Unique in no one else can be where you are
At the exact same time.

A sneeze,
A smile,
Stay here for a while.
You are safe.
You are home.
You are alive.
Welcome back.

The Only Currency is Now

Launiopoko, Maui

The only currency is Now.
No stockpiling high the moments.
If you don't own it, who else will?

Life's thrills don't happen in the future,
Down yonder,
What's the point of withering away, pondering
What has occurred or where you need to be
At a quarter til…when?

What's more beautiful than Now?

To what extent has judgement tilted your brows?
Fix that smile, it's upside down

When all there is is bright heavenly light,
Out of sight, out of mind, right?

Cosmically Cosmopolitan

Pūpūkea, O'ahu

Looking across the sky
Dreams unfold in untimed line
What's to come and what's come to pass
The Now is here at last.

Running when resurrects the sky
Running until opposites fly
Pushing to get on island time
Is pushing away the island's sublime

Heaven comes to those who wait
While we are trying to maintain our gold in weight
Hitting the gas pedal on cosmic fate
Trying to be early when you're a person of late

Running shoeless across desert plain
Running through the picture frame
Framing questions to validate our own answers
When our answers are our own cancers

Cosmically cosmopolitan
Is what I want to be
A responsible galactic being
Seeing to see

Freeing voices follow me
Spreading Alōha patiently
Unfolding as the moments unfold,
The laundromat of old souls.

Spinning counterclockwise from the clock
On this ticking time bomb rock
Marching to the celestial beat
Jumping into unknown fog with two feet

Come along and walk with thee
Oscillate among constellations we can barely see
Why not? Reconnect for a while
Maybe I'll even make you smile

Infantile auric sight
Energy fields shine so bright
When bias and fear drip, drop away
Like God's tears on a rainy day

Cosmically cosmopolitan
Is what I want to be
A responsible galactic being
Being to be

Tiptoeing tight ropes to the moon
Roses blossom, tulips bloom
Consumed by the plume of synchronicity
Opening mind's doors to serendipity

Astral travelling to stellar states
No getting clammy at the pearly gates
Here awaits the land of the true and free
Way more obvious than what we've been programmed to see

As we row our boats to the base of the stream
Letting ourselves slip into the flow's golden mean
As the cool, crisp waters wash over our souls
Magnetizing left and right brain poles

Subtle perspective tweaks
Give glimpses of the peak
Not something up upon you can sneak
Ageless carbon legends of Celts and Greeks

As this consciousness dissipates with evaporative ease
Transcendence gives thanks as long as we say please

Surrender to divine but see it as true
The mirror in me is the mirror in you!

Cosmically cosmopolitan
Is what I want to be
A responsible galactic being
Freeing to free

Be a Tree

Pa'ia, Maui

Be a Tree.
This tree is stratified in the sense
That its fruits are shared
With the ants and the squirrels
As much as the giraffes and the birds.

How can we be able to communicate
On all levels
And maintain this tree-energy?

By providing people with what they need at the moment.

No squirrel or giraffe is better or worse than one another,
But different in their needs.

We all eat from the tree,
Breathe from the tree,
And are the tree.

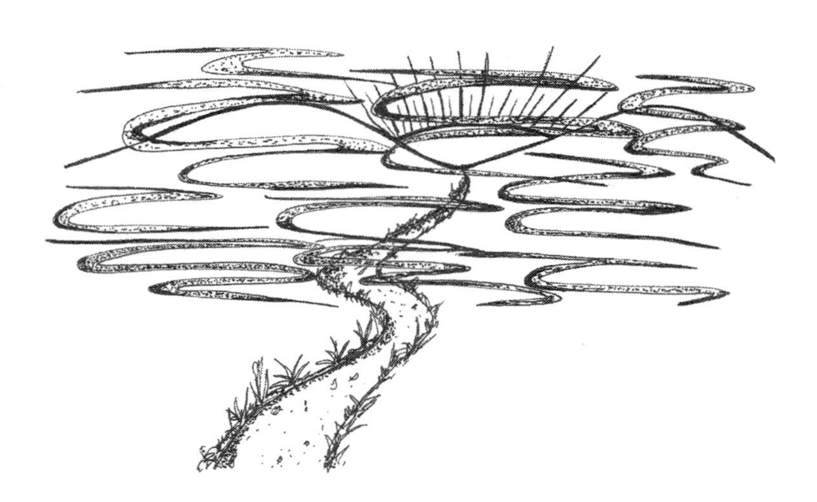

Fog

Makawao, Maui

Fog,
The mystical bridge,
Between the here and the yonder.

Between our past and our future.
Preventing us from seeing our intended destination.

What happens when we disappear into the mist?
What's on the other side?

Regardless,
We must cross through the fog.

With limited vision,
And hope,
And a light-Heart.

We must have faith
That on the other side
There will be a beautiful sunset,
Illuminating the sky
And the clouds.

This clears all the doubt
From our minds,
About why we walked through
In the first place.

Savior

Kula, Maui

Am I looking for a savior?
To save me from me?
Someone who I can confide,
My deepest secrets which I want to hide from myself?

Am I looking for a savior?
To help lift me up when I am feeling down?
Someone who can cheer me up with a smile,
When I am fooling myself into being sad?

Am I looking for a savior?
To protect me from self-harm?
Someone who with a sword and a shield,
Can block the arrows from my mind directed at my Heart?

Am I looking for a savior?
To water my roots when they're dry?
Pruning my gnarled branches,
When they reach out and scratch passerbyes?

Am I looking for a savior?
To lay with me when I am lonely?
Hug me and tell me everything is going to be alright,
Even if it isn't?

Am I looking for a savior?
A knightess and stallion steed?
Someone to bandage me up,
When I can't clot my wounds that bleed?

Am I looking for a savior?
To challenge me and help me grow?
Providing constructive critiques on subtle observations,
Pointing out the flaws which deep down I already know?

Am I looking for a savior?
To feed me when I am hungry?
Providing nourishment,
If I don't want to digest what's to come?

Am I looking for a savior?
To validate my self-worth?
If no one else sees my value,
Does that mean I am cursed?

Am I looking for a savior?
To guide my sailboat through the stars?
Stopping by Mercury in retrograde,
Fly-by Aphrodite and even past Mars?

Am I looking for a savior?
To make my life easy and convenient?
Someone to grease the rails
Of this archaic rollercoaster of my mind?

Am I looking for a savior?
To find me when I'm dead?
Make sure I navigate through the after-life safely,
If Anubis denies me at the threshold?

Am I looking for a savior?
To save me from me?
Someone who reminds me of myself,
Someone to help me be free?

Chapter 6: Africa

I first moved to Cameroon in 2012 after I had graduated from Northeastern University. I had finished my classes in Valencia, Spain and then on behalf of a project that was beginning named Jola Venture, went over with a group of recent graduates to a village named Bali-Nyonga close to the large city of Bamenda. From 2012 until 2019 I spent almost 1.5 years between Cameroon and Ghana.

I was not writing during most of my time in Cameroon but these three poems are from my recent time in Ghana in 2019.

Dreams of an African Child
Keta, Ghana

Deep in the eyes of an African child
I see a land of kings and queens
Adorned with cowrie and beads
Gold and opals
Plates full of bananas and papaya
Ripe for the celebrations that lay ahead

Deep in the eyes of an African child
I see suffering beyond what I can imagine
Pains from the generations
Passing through the gates of no return
Watching as their homes drift away,
Sold by their own chiefs

Deep in the eyes of an African child
I see absolute joy
Freedom and laughter as they chase after cars
Giggling in the bush with the goats
By the roadside
Heels kicking up dust as they speed up the sprint
Wonder and happiness abounding

Deep in the eyes of an African child
I see genius and ingenuity
Kites made of palm and old plastic bags
Car horn that beep from the windshield fluid handle
Calabash food preservers
And vibrant Kente fabric that can last
One hundred years

Deep in the eyes of an African child
I see hope and pride
For them to rule and manage their own lands
Free from weapons and colonialist sponsored rebels

Galamseys and neo-imperialism
Thieves stealing the wealth from the jungle
Leaving waters dirty
And lands dead and barren

Deep in the eyes of an African child
I see me
Me without borders and color
Spirit connecting through the eye of the needle
Soul drenched in compassion
and acceptance
And Love
And a new wave of being

Fishing

Elmina, Ghana

We out here fishing for clues
Amidst the blues –
Only fools can snooze
As we move
So it is in the wins and the lose
Losing ourselves is something we choose
When we skip the noose
Slipping loose
Towards freedom's pursuit
In the being and not the do

Sleep, Darling

Akosombo, Ghana

Sleep, darling
Rest those eyes
They've seen so much
Sometimes they need to just be
Covered in silken skin
Darkness within
Silence and colors spin
You deserve it
Rainbow soul kaleidoscope
Who else can heal you but you?
We don't need this or that
That's the work of the Mad Hat
Trying to sort through it all
Label and place
Space
It is safe
Within this race you can breathe
Let your body be the sieve
Through which you filter the light
Gentle and without a fight
It'll be all right
Good night.

Ryan J. Kemp

has worked in, lived in, and traveled to over forty-five countries in the past eight years. He has consulted with the ex-Prime Minister of Cameroon, Philémon Yang, to implement rural infrastructure initiatives to help farming communities cut down on food spoilage, studied Tibetan Buddhism at a monastery in Nepal, drafted MOUs for the Minister of Energy in Myanmar working towards renewable energy independence, and lived and worked on intentional communities and permaculture farms throughout Hawai'i, the Caribbean, and Central America. He is a certified YTT-200 hour Ashtanga Yoga teacher, Ayurvedic dietician and masseuse, published children's book author, and poet. His most recent book is titled *The Age of Separation*, and is available on Amazon. He currently resides on the Big Island of Hawai'i.

Made in the USA
Middletown, DE
10 October 2020

21568518R00108